My Cody

My Cody

His Cancer, Our Faith & God's Love

JACQUELYN NICOLE WILDE EUBANKS

MY CODY
His Cancer, Our Faith & God's Love

ISBN   978-1-5445-2377-4 *Hardcover*
       978-1-5445-2375-0 *Paperback*
       978-1-5445-2376-7 *Ebook*

Graphics
Kate Phelps with Kate Phelps Photography
Candice Baise with Candice Baise Photography
David Warren with Dwarren Photography
Diana Laura García Márquez with Tropics

This book is dedicated
to my perfect Lord, Jesus Christ,
and my beloved, late husband,
Cody Keon Eubanks.

Cody,

*I'll never understand in this lifetime why you were taken from
me. I know you were never mine to begin with, but I thought we
had so much left to see and do together. And although I won't
understand, I have peace in God's plan. My heart breaks over
and over again daily at my new reality without you, but I don't
feel that you are far away. My cup still overflows with blessings
that I believe you have your hand in. Thank you for still taking
care of me, darling. Thank you for showing me the deepest
form of love that my flesh can actually comprehend. I miss your
physical presence on this earth drastically, but oftentimes I
find humor that death thought it could part us. No way. Jesus
conquered the grave! Thank you for all the amazing memories
and teaching me so very much. You have truly given me the love
of a lifetime. I will always love you.*

Jesus,

*Thank you for aggressively pursuing my heart and calling
me closer despite the pain in my chest. I know You are real,
and I know You to be true. I dedicate not only this book, but
everything that I am to you.*

CONTENTS

PREFACE

Writing this book perhaps saved me from sinking into the deepest form of depression imaginable. I was only twenty-three years old when my world was suddenly changed forever. Journaling gave me comfort in being able to express and process the changes going on all around me on my own time, instead of giving in to the pressures, preconceived notions, and expectations that the world gives.

I cannot take credit for the supernatural power and strength Christ has given me during the immense grieving period I was in while writing this book. Without the Lord's grace, mercy, guidance, and provision, losing the love of my life surely would have leveled me in an unrecoverable way. It is in Him that I have been able to *see* and find peace in healing. If I can recognize His goodness and experience His love in my absolute lowest valley, surely you can, too! One's journey is as unique as a fingerprint, and I encourage all to seek refuge in Him.

Xoxo

—*Jackie*

chapter one

June 10, 2020

It had been a really, really long day. All the details from the past twenty-four hours were just a blur. There seemed to be a lot of these days lately where the minutes felt like weeks, and the hours felt like months. An overwhelmed feeling paralyzed our mental state as we slowly started settling in for the night. We were beyond exhausted, but our minds drifted with wonder about the unknown.

Only a few short days ago, my husband and I were happily celebrating our one-year wedding anniversary with not a single care in the world—June 1, 2019. The most monumental day of our entire existence thus far was when our two flesh became one under God and all who were present there. It was truly the most magical day of my entire life, and it couldn't have been more perfect. We celebrated the Big One by blindfolding my groom to surprise him with an adventure back to our wedding venue, Cason's Cove. There we enjoyed a picnic together to indulge the same meal we catered in on our wedding night. We exchanged anniversary gifts, then walked around the venue for a while, reminiscing about our perfect day. This place is extra special to me because it is owned by close family friends. I had spent many weekends and summers in high school, working and helping with the events held there, including other weddings. Going back and taking a stroll down memory lane, side by side with my husband, was so refreshing and good for our souls.

Other than the global COVID-19 pandemic of 2020, we were *thriving* and abundantly blessed by God with a wonderful marriage and extraordinary, supportive family and friends. We were making attempts at growing our family of two, seeking membership and involvement at our beloved church, and preparing for an exciting move into our first house. Both of our businesses were booming incredibly, our finances for once were pretty solid, and we were only a pinch away from becoming a debt-free family. In our own fantasy bubble, everything was falling into place for us, and our lives together seemed as close to perfect as this world could get. To treat ourselves and celebrate with a cherry on top of some pretty exciting milestones, my husband was getting enthused for us to purchase that blacked-out Ford F-150 truck he had always dreamed about outright buying. Black wheels, black trim, tinted windows—the whole nine yards. A reality with no car payments or debt was a huge goal for us and our family's mission. Cody and I had been extremely blessed in all avenues in such little time. Life was good. In fact, life was too good almost to the point of becoming too comfortable.

But now, my husband's health had taken a drastic turn for the worse. Neither of us knew what was wrong yet, but his symptoms such as rapid weight loss, unexplainable fatigue, vomiting episodes, and achiness in his bones and joints were becoming more and more frequent. He kept expressing how he just didn't feel like himself. We had been warned by medical professionals that whatever it was, wasn't good, and would be caught much too late. And I was terrified.

After much time had passed of us mindlessly watching who-knows-what on Netflix, my better half began to snore. He really hadn't been sleeping well for months now. As I looked over at him sleeping peacefully, I tried to muster up the strength to smile. I was so thankful he was able to rest, but how in the world was I supposed to sleep knowing what I now knew? My mind was racing about the potential days ahead. I was numb and felt helpless.

After letting my fleshly thoughts get the best of me for a while, I paused the TV, sat up in bed, crossed my legs, and positioned myself towards his direction. And there he was. So peaceful, yet not himself. Seemingly invincible, yet delicate, too. I wanted absolutely nothing more than to take his place.

I gently pulled back the covers and laid my hands softly on his belly. The protrusion under the surface of his skin there frightened me. I couldn't help but begin to pray. "Lord . . . Lord . . . Lord . . ." I said quietly. How could this be? I just knew we had so much more to see and do together. Imagining him significantly ill or leaving this world wasn't possible or even an option for me. Certainly, this was all just a dream that I would wake up from at any moment. I longed for a miracle. "Lord . . . Lord . . . Lord," I continued to mutter over and over again. I was searching, but

I couldn't find any other words. At that moment, I had forgotten the rest of the entire English language. What had we done wrong to deserve such torment? The tears were now flowing, and they weren't soaking up. My heart *ached*. "Lord . . . Lord . . . Lord." I repeated His name at least one hundred times and was lost for any other words. My soft weeping was becoming hard to control, but gracefully our God knows the desires of our hearts and any of our thoughts before they are released off the tips of our tongues.

After much time had passed of me pleading on behalf of the unknown, I faintly heard my husband's head readjust on the pillow.

Out of nowhere, he boldly said, "I hear you!"

I was startled and quickly opened my eyes. My voice had been so quiet, there was no way he could've heard me praying. While trying to make out his face in the darkness of the room, our gazes locked. I apologetically jumped back, knowing that it must have seemed a bit creepy to be hunched over him in the middle of the night. *Oops!*

"I'm sorry, I'm sorry! I was just praying over your body," I pleaded.

I felt so bad that I had woken him from his much-needed sleep. And yet, without a response or any other movement, he dozed right back to sleep just as swiftly as he had woken up. Odd. Once the snoring resumed, so did my praying. The Spirit flowed and so did my words to the Father. This time, Christ was able to get more out of me other than "Lord." This time, I felt *different.*

Once the tears gradually faded to a halt, my body begged me for sleep. I forced myself to remain upright and keep praying, but eventually the exhaustion won. Still feeling like five hundred pounds of bricks sat on my chest, I restlessly rolled over, got somewhat comfy, and listened to the sound of the television as background noise for a while to help me drift to sleep. Honestly, I didn't want to face the next day, but I had to stay strong for my Cody.

The next morning, I slowly made my way downstairs to find my husband sitting in his recliner, studying for a big work exam he had coming up. Cody had been studying for his Series 7 license for several months now. This certification would then allow him to be fully licensed to do all investment types, and his determination to once again level up in his career was inspiring. Unfortunately, his unwarranted health conditions had become a major distraction to this goal he was aiming to reach.

"Good morning, I'm so sorry about last night," I began. "I didn't mean to startle you!" Making my way to have a seat on the couch beside him, I noticed that Cody looked puzzled.

"What are you talking about?" he asked.

"Oh! Me praying over you while you slept. You know?"

His face gave it away that he truly had no clue what I was talking about. So I began to explain the sequence of events and how *he heard me.* Cody patiently listened and stared at me in confusion.

"Cody, don't play with me. You spoke to me. Don't you remember?" I exclaimed, both playful and astonished.

I couldn't understand how he didn't remember that. He had spoken the words "I hear you" so confidently. There had been no groan in his voice like he had just woken up. His voice was clear and smooth. We even made eye contact and locked eyes. I knew he had spoken to me.

Cody, still trying to process what I told him, said, "Jackie, last night I got the best night of rest that I have gotten in months. I woke up only one time to pee. I didn't even hear you talking or the sound of the TV. I don't remember any of what you're telling me."

We both instantly got goosebumps, or "chicken titties" as Cody liked to call them.

Who had really spoken to me the night before? My spirit was super receptive in that moment to who really told me "I hear you." I knew that the Mighty Man in heaven Himself had told me that He heard me through my husband. Before we even received the official diagnosis, Jesus was hearing our prayers. And I strongly believe He was already answering them, too.

chapter two

Meet Cody

His story begins in Sebring, Florida, where he was born and raised. Cody's biological father wasn't around much while Cody was growing up, so he was solely raised by his young mother and stepdad. Cody was the oldest of his mother's four boys and somewhere else in the ranking of his birth-dad's seven other children. I had been told many times by several family members that Cody was always super independent, kept to himself, had a brilliant mind of his own, and didn't require much observation or correction. He was well beyond his years in maturity and overall filled with so much joy.

Cody's family wasn't as financially blessed as others. He would tell me of times when they would go a week straight eating only rice and canned pork and beans because it was the only affordable food at the time. Or how at the beginning of each school year, he wore his grown uncle's baggy, hand-me-down clothes to school because they couldn't afford anything else.

Every Christmas, Cody would remind me of the time where he had to give back his already-opened Christmas present because "Santa" miscalculated it in the budget. Santa had brought four remote control toy cars for the four brothers, but Santa and Mrs. Claus had not been on the same page financially. His parents decided that it would be in the family's best interest if two of the toy cars went back to the North Pole. Unfortunately, Cody's Christmas present was taken right out of his hands. This story still haunted him in his adult years, because the disappointment he felt was devastating. But even as a young child, he understood this sacrifice.

Despite lacking material possessions, anytime the church building doors were open, his mom made sure her boys were in attendance. Cody remembers spending every Tuesday night, Thursday night, and twice on Sundays between those double doors. He grew up respectfully obeying the teachings of the old religious principles, practices, rituals, and rules. Cody recalled long days seated in those pews where he was struck with the fear of God Almighty. He would later learn that the Big Man upstairs isn't confined into a small box, but that He exudes love, and His reign is limitless.

Every family has their fair share of dysfunction, but the perspective that Cody's gave him at such a young age was fascinating. He had been granted the gift of discernment and wisdom from the Holy Spirit much sooner than most, and he excelled in his self-discipline. When he would reminisce and reflect on his upbringing, he was grateful for being exposed to a fair share of chaos early on, because it showed him what he didn't want to be like before he knew what he did want to be like.

Ultimately, seeing his immediate family struggle financially and several of his extended relatives wrestle with the same issue as well as drug addictions, theft behaviors, and physical violence inspired Cody to strive in breaking his family's generational curse. Cody wanted much more for himself than his hometown had to offer. With the crime rate in Sebring rising, he knew if he had stayed there, he wouldn't become the man he was aspiring to be. So at fifteen years old, he asked his mom if he could move to Franklin, Kentucky, with his aunt and her two small children. She answered him with a quick yes, and he left all he had known to create a new life for himself.

In Franklin, Cody quickly found a part-time job at a local fast-food restaurant and joined the football, basketball, and track and field programs at his new school. Thriving in all things athletic, maintaining stellar grades, and keeping up a phenomenal work ethic came naturally to him. He loved to learn and embrace challenges. To no one's surprise, he soon began to dominate on the football field. Cody began making the front page of the newspaper quite often. "Eubanks Does It Again!" The crowds that gathered on game day absolutely adored him. The whole town was in awe of the new kid from Florida drawing this much attention to their small-town football team. Even with the spotlight on him for the first time in his life, his spirit remained meek and humble.

After high school, Cody accepted a scholarship to continue his passion for football and to run track at Campbellsville University in Campbellsville, Kentucky. Oh, and he flourished! On the football field, he played wide receiver and kickoff returner on special teams. On the track and field team, he competed in the 100m and 200m dash and participated in the 4x100m and 4x200m relays. The Campbellsville Tigers couldn't brag enough about this kid from the South! Boys will be boys, so he did have his fair share of rambunctious college stories, but nothing too crazy that made headlines in the local newspaper. Cody pitched a tent on the dean's list and assured that his grades came first. He was highly favored by his teachers, abundantly cherished by his coaches, and deeply loved to this day by his college group of friends.

After four years of much growth, he walked the line with his bachelor's degree in Business Administration. Cody was the first college attendee in his immediate family, let alone college graduate! If I could time-travel, I would be honored to go back to witness this extremely rewarding moment in his life. My hero. My inspiration. Want to know something absolutely amazing? Cody didn't stop there!

After graduation, Cody decided to test the waters and try out for a semi-pro, arena football team in Louisville, Kentucky, called Louisville Fire. Louisville Fire was blessed by his skillset, warm enthusiasm, and ability to be a great team player. That opportunity and experience was incredible and all; but after a while, Cody felt that it was time to hang up the cleats and go back to school. After one season spent in Louisville, he returned to Campbellsville University, where he earned his master's degree in Business Administration. This man was hands down someone to be proud of. And this was only the beginning!

Once freed from twenty-one years of schooling, Cody accepted a general manager position with Bluegrass Cellular in Bowling Green, Kentucky, where he specialized in technology sales. Cody really enjoyed his new job and began networking within his new town. His employees joked that he ran a very tight ship around there and was rather strict, but they never doubted how much Cody cared for each of them and took pride in his store's honorable reputation.

The years came and went until his season at Bluegrass ended, too. During the course of those several years, he managed to create a wonderful name for himself within the community, and he gained many meaningful friendships. After much thought and soul-searching, Cody built up a desire to serve his country by dedicating his life to the United States Air Force. He was super eager to enlist and began the enrollment process, but one day a close friend approached him about a career opportunity in financial services with a reputable company. This decision wasn't an easy one to make. Yet with Cody now in his late twenties and having suffered from football injuries to his shoulder and knee, he found it best to stick around good ole Bowling Green and pursue this career path. He accepted an opening with AIG Financial as an insurance agent. Cody loved how this career stimulated his mind and pushed him out of his comfort zone. He loved meeting new faces and having a major impact on other families' financial decisions. I often teased him about being part calculator. Someone enjoying numbers, math, counting, and equations that much couldn't be sane.

In 2016, still doing what he loved and impacting more and more people day by day, he switched companies from AIG Financial to a Christian-based company called Thrivent Financial, where his soul still resides today. What better way to help bless families and organizations financially than to share it with Christ-like perspectives and principles!

Cody was a remarkable man. Those who knew him were his biggest fans, and he was a blessing to everyone he encountered, friend or stranger. He loved volunteering, especially when it came to the underprivileged youth. He was a walking sponge and wanted to soak up any bit of knowledge from anyone willing to teach him a thing or two. He set his bar as limitless, because he knew he could accomplish anything he set his mind and heart to. He was a rare breed, indeed.

Words would never be able to convey his characteristics and attributes. He was truly unique and a son of the King! His integrity, passion, hunger, and thirst for Christ radiated out of his being. His faithfulness to his Maker, wife, family, and friends was like none other. He was *dangerously loyal*. His sense of humor brought laughter that made your tummy hurt, and his stories warmed the souls of those who would listen. This man had a heart of gold and would have given the shirt off of his back to anyone in a heartbeat. Without thought or question, he went out of his way to make people feel welcome and wanted. He was a lover of all people and genuine all the way through.

It was in his nature to meet people where they were in life. He didn't seek attention from this world but strived to defend what's right through the eyes of Yahweh. At the same time, he was the most levelheaded, mentally sound person that I ever knew. He had no expectation for life other than to live as Jesus would. His honesty, thoughtfulness, strength, compassion, and wisdom inspired me and many others so much. It was evident that he was devoted to making this world a better place. Thankfully, he put his trust and worries into the lap of our Jehovah Rapha. He could have been living in the midst of a nightmare, yet no one would have ever known it. This was my Cody.

chapter three

June 15, 2020

I woke up on this Monday morning paralyzed from head to toe. We had been holding our breath all weekend and plus some for this wretched day. Now that it was finally here for us to sit one on one with the doctor to discuss Cody's biopsy results, I prayed for more time and begged that this was all just a dream. I longed to be taken back to just months ago, when my husband seemed to be extremely healthy. How did he go from hiking miles at a time, annihilating my butt in one-on-one tennis, and waking up every morning at 5:00 a.m. to train for triathlons with his buddies—to being too drained before taking a single step?

Cody noticed a shift in his health in the fall of 2019, shortly after our wedding. He went to his primary doctor in September with concerns that he didn't feel like himself and that "something was wrong." His doctor conducted all of the blood work simply to say, "It's nothing of major concern." Instead of digging deeper and getting to the root of the problem, he prescribed some medication for Cody's noticeable fatigue and achy symptoms. Fast-forward to January of 2020, and he went back to the doctor with horrible acid reflux issues and complaints of the medication not working. He was then prescribed a different medication for energy and the acid reflux, before being sent home. Knowing his body and that something else wasn't right, he sought out a different doctor in March for a fresh set of eyes. When the new bloodwork came back, this doctor raised concerns about Cody's kidney levels. They were elevated, but why? He was merely given more medication to suppress his symptoms.

Around the first quarter of 2020, COVID-19 began to rage not only throughout the United States but globally. Cody hardly felt the benefits of any of the medication he was taking, and he was persistent in saying he felt tired and not like himself. I remember one evening in particular as we were settling in for the night, I laid my head down on the pillow and curled up close to him in bed. He turned sideways facing me, looked deep into the pit of my soul with those big, beautiful chocolate eyes of his, and slowly said, "Jackie, I am *tired*." He looked at me for understanding, his voice weak yet stern. I believed my husband, but I didn't know what to possibly think or do. He still looked healthy despite the weight he had lost—he'd been trying to lose weight, anyways. I said something reassuring like, "Honey, only you know your body better than anyone else. If you want me to fight for you, I will. You just have to tell me. We're in this together, so let's get to the bottom of why you're not feeling like yourself." I encouraged him to let us seek out more doctors, but at that point two physicians had already told us that it was nothing. We'd trusted them as trained, licensed professionals; we'd trusted the information and medicine they had given us.

In early April of 2020, we noticed Cody's belly beginning to protrude. Yet unless you had COVID-19 symptoms, obtaining a doctor's appointment at that time was nearly impossible. Everything was shutting down, and facilities weren't seeing patients unless it was a life-threatening emergency. Cody didn't seem too concerned and neither did the medical professionals, but this was an emergency to me! The soonest anyone could get us in for an ultrasound was late May. And the rest is history.

As to be expected, I wasn't sleeping very well due to anxiety, nerves, and fear. I had been spiritually fasting from meals for three days prior. My purpose in doing this fast was to devote all of my attention towards good news, positive thoughts, healing energy, and the love of Christ. Anytime I thought of my fleshly hunger, I strived in filling my soul with the goodness of the Lord. Needless to say, my body was brutally numb and zapped from being overwhelmed. I struggled to pull myself together, but I knew time stopped for no man. *Chop, chop! Let's get moving.*

With that morning seemingly moving in slow motion, I did all I knew how to do. I prayed. I prayed for no cancer, but also prayed for peace over me and my husband. I prayed to let us walk with grace if this was the path the Lord had chosen for us. I prayed for us never to lose the faith or take our eyes off of God's sovereignty. He takes care of His children. He makes no mistakes.

I had been listening to the testimony of Joel Osteen's mom about her healing from cancer. Dodie swore up and down that prayer was the root to her healing.

So, when my husband came downstairs about an hour before the appointment, I followed her lead. I led Cody to the couch and told him to have a seat. I brought out his Bible, which had his name, *Cody Eubanks*, engraved on it. I placed it on the ground in front of him, where it was now between us. I gently slid off his socks and asked him to stand on the Word. On my knees before my husband and the Bible, I cupped my hands around his feet and ankles and began to pray aloud, "Lord, we are standing on Your Word. No matter what the doctors or anyone says about our future today, we are standing on Your promises. We will listen to what You say about this situation, Father God. You are the Great Physician. You are the Mighty Healer. You are the doctor of life, and we breathe You in. Thank you for pursuing our hearts, Jesus."

Everything about this sacred moment empowered us for the day, and even months ahead.

Neither Cody nor I said a single word during the car ride to the doctor's office. We listened to the worship music softly playing in the background while holding hands like we always did in the car. I drove as usual, simply because I get carsick when riding shotgun. Cody liked to tease me that he was my Miss Daisy from the 1989 *Driving Miss Daisy* film. He grew to like me chauffeuring him around. This ten-minute drive across town felt like ten hours. I felt extremely nauseous even though I wasn't the passenger. Do you know that feeling when you are sweating and shivering at the same time? Yeah . . . I was ready to hurl.

We pulled up at the Graves Gilbert Clinic, where his biopsy results awaited on the other side of those large, glass, double doors. Neither one of us was truly ready to get out of the car. With certainty, I assured him that no matter what the doctor said, I was *all* in, and he could forever count on me to be his helpmate. I reminded him of all the promises I made to him and God on our wedding day. For better or for worse, in sickness and in health, I vowed to never leave his side.

We took a deep breath and began our journey inside. Locking hands, we refused to let one another go. His grip was extra tight, but I didn't mind one bit. As soon as we stepped inside, the brisk cool air from the large building sent chills up my spine. I wondered if anyone could hear my heartbeat, because my heart was pounding out of my chest. I was beyond nervous, but I couldn't let Cody see me bent out of shape.

The doctor saw us immediately. His demeanor was off, and his face was flushed like he had just seen a ghost. I took in every detail of the space around us, every word spoken, until he said the words, "I am sorry to be the one to tell you this, Cody, but you have cancer." After that, everything slowly began to fade, and I swore I was beginning to lose consciousness. I could not believe it, and I was ready to wake up from the disastrous dream I had been living. My life felt like it was ending as it flashed before my eyes.

Instantly, I glanced over to see my husband's reaction. Nothing. Cody didn't seem bothered. I just assumed he was in pure shock. I wanted to cry, but before I knew it, the doctor was choking up and his nurse was weeping puddles. After having previous encounters with Cody, they felt nothing short of genuine concern for our family. Next thing I knew, Cody was consoling each of us by assuring everyone that he would fight this, and everything would be okay. He kept it together well. Because he was strong, I was able to be strong and keep it together, too. His reassurance and confidence filled me with hope. To this day, I wonder what really crossed his mind in that room or how he was truly feeling when given the news. Certainly, he was fazed and possibly terrified, but he never outwardly showed it.

That afternoon, my husband was diagnosed with an insanely aggressive form of Hepatocellular Carcinoma. Most of the events afterwards are foggy to my memory now. I briefly remember us going home and telling Cody's mother the news, since she had come into town to visit the night before. Also, Cody and I prepared ourselves to meet with our assigned oncologist that afternoon to discuss our game plan in proceeding with treatment. But the rest of the day draws a blank for me. We were in the process of moving from our apartment into our first house, so boxes were stacked everywhere. I felt claustrophobic and needed to breathe. I longed for comfort that only Christ could provide. Witnessing Cody's strength, composure, and faith seemed to be the only thing holding me together.

Only one other moment from that day clearly stands out to me. That afternoon my younger brother, Jacob, called attempting to console me and Cody with love and support. I'm not sure what he was thinking or if he was thinking at all, but on this day, he decided to share some important news with us.

Jacob told us that he was expecting a baby. A precious, innocent baby boy. He had been keeping this a secret for some time now. The mother was pretty far along, and the baby would arrive in September. She and Jacob had met at a party one night, and they did not keep in touch after that. She'd reached out a few months later to let him know that he was going to be a father. My heart was throbbing upon hearing this news. Until now, Cody and I had been trying to conceive.

Although conceiving wasn't happening immediately like we had hoped, we were excited and eager to become parents! We had been making all the proper precautions to ensure that our children would be raised comfortably and safely. And we were giddy over the thought of bringing my parents their first grandbaby. We knew this would bring our families so much joy! We were ready to enter into the season of parenthood, and we knew God would bless us with a beautiful child when He saw fit. However, our "plan" wasn't His plan.

The waves of emotions on this day were surreal. Fear, peace, sorrow, confusion, and stillness. Feeling loved and then pitied, experiencing weakness and confidence in the same moment. Shock and jealousy to comfort and hope. Potentially looking death in the eye to the thrill of experiencing a new life. The news of our soon-to-be nephew made us smile, but also broke our hearts at the same time. What a day. My husband, the love of my life, just got the worst news anyone could hear, which would change our family and our lives drastically. We didn't know what to think or how to feel. We didn't know how to proceed or how to sit completely still.

Needless to say, we had to put our complete trust in the Lord, because it was certain that we were not in control. As difficult as not being in control was, Cody encouraged me to control my thoughts on how I viewed this trial. So, I instilled these thoughts into my heart and repeated them over and over: *His plan is always used for His own good, even when we may not see it right now. We vowed to be His willing vessels and to be used for the expansion of His kingdom. We absolutely still love Him, rain or shine. There is a reason for everything that He allows. And He makes no mistakes for those of us who believe in Him.*

chapter four

How We Met

I will never forget the day I met Cody Keon Eubanks: March 23, 2017. I had just broken up with my high school sweetheart the day before. The breakup was inevitable and a long time coming, but we won't get too far down that rabbit hole. After much soul searching and growth, I simply realized that we were two completely different people who had different priorities in life, and that's okay! I felt confident in this decision, and the day was going great.

At the time, I had been volunteering as a track and field coach at my former high school, South Warren, in Bowling Green, Kentucky. This sport had been my passion for many years. If it weren't for a pretty bad ankle injury right before my first practice, I would have continued pole vaulting and long jumping collegiately at Western Kentucky University. It was a tough pill to swallow at the time, but I understood even then that everything happens for a reason.

On that Thursday afternoon, I was on the ten-minute drive from my parents' house to another local high school across town, to coach my student-athletes at a track meet. This route passed through the small community of Plano, located on the outskirts of Bowling Green. The sun was shining, and the air was brisk. It was a great day to spend the evening on the track! Usually I drove a small, white 2003 Mercedes Benz, but since it had been having mechanical issues, my dad let me swap it out for his big, solid, old Yukon. This would soon turn out to be a miracle.

Anyone who lives in Plano knows about the "S curve." This stretch consists of two sharp curves that require extreme caution. As I was leaving my parents and heading into the first curve towards town, a guy rear-ended my car like a bat outta hell! Upon the initial hit, I lost control of my vehicle and spun into oncoming traffic. Unbelievably, my vehicle dodged the other cars and swung right off of the road, over some decent-size boulders, and peacefully landed in a field beside a church. Talk about frightening!

While getting rear-ended, my very first thought was that God was punishing me for breaking that sweet boy's heart the day before. Yet I later learned that He was just making this day *extra* memorable; in fact, evil was trying to disrupt what was to come! Within minutes a fire truck, several police cars, an ambulance, and my parents had flooded the scene. Thankfully, neither I nor the man who hit me was badly hurt, but it was evident that both vehicles were totaled. If it were not for me driving the Yukon that day, I would've been seriously injured. Christ never ceases to amaze me. His angels had truly been watching us.

Despite the mild frustration of the paramedics and my parents, I resisted going to the hospital. Rationally, I should've gone— my health was more important, and my track kiddos would've been just fine without me for one day—but something larger than that was telling me that I could not miss *this* track meet.

After much badgering, my dad ended up driving me the rest of the way to the meet. He was persistent the entire way that it wasn't too late to swing over to the emergency room. No thanks! Totally feeling like it was high school again and he was dropping me off for my own competition, I scurried over to the coach's circle where the other coaches and officials had started without me. When this meeting concluded, I made my way over to the long jump pit to put my bags down, greet the athletes, and take a seat. *Whew!* The adrenaline was now beginning to wear off. I felt like crap. Why had I come?

As I was sitting there in the grass, trying to keep my head from spinning off, an approximately six-foot-tall, dark, and rather handsome man with a gigantic smile approached me. He was wearing an old ball cap, hoodie, and sweatpants along with a grin from ear to ear. I stood up to shake his hand and introduce myself, too. His name was Cody. I couldn't help but notice that he was full of passion and charisma.

He began to tell me that he was a volunteer coach as well for Franklin Simpson High School in Franklin, Kentucky, and how he had competed on their team years ago, too.

"I was standing on the other side of the track watching you interact with your team. Do you think you could teach me a thing or two?" he spoke.

Cody wanted my help with his jumpers since he didn't specialize in jumping events—his specialties were in individual races and relay events. He went on and on bragging about the talent Franklin Simpson possessed, but he didn't know how to properly take them to the next level.

"Any other day I would gladly demonstrate and take you up on helping with your athletes, just not today," I replied.

I didn't want to offend him by declining, so I took out my phone to show him pictures of the wreck I had just been in.

"This happened about thirty minutes ago. Honestly, I shouldn't even be here. I feel terrible," I explained.

He was shocked! "Woah! For what it's worth, I think you look great," he said.

At the time, I totally did not think too much of his compliment. He offered to get me a bottled water from the concession stand and to let him know if there was anything he could do to make me more comfortable. He showed genuine concern, was so friendly, and super easy to talk to. He was one of those people I felt like I had known forever.

When the meet had begun, we hovered around the long jump pit for the next couple of hours. The atmosphere was so welcoming among our two teams. Cody and I were not specifically entertaining one other, but we had the same objectives, so we naturally stayed close to each other. At first, I could tell he was listening in when I would give my kids feedback or critique their form. It was amusing watching how observant he was and eager to learn for the best interest of his kids. He analyzed my athletes and even pulled his athletes aside to watch and study their performances. Occasionally he would have me watch his athletes' form, and he would ask me questions or to provide feedback on their work. By the end of the night, he was cheering on my kids, I was cheering on his kids, his athletes were cheering on my athletes, and my athletes were cheering on his athletes. It was a fun night of friendly competition.

Cody's humility really stood out to me in particular. There's not many grown men or former athletes who would seek advice from someone they just met—let alone a female rival coach who is young, meek in spirit, and five-foot-three in height. Right before we parted ways for the night, we said our good jobs and goodbyes. After walking several feet away from one another, I glanced back at the pit to find him still staring at me. I never in a million years would have thought that man from that day would turn out to be my soul mate.

chapter five

Strength and Perseverance

When we received the initial diagnosis on June 15, 2020, the largest tumor in his liver measured 19.5 x 14.2 x 10.4 centimeters, comparable to the size of a large cantaloupe or small watermelon. Scans also spotted several other tumors ranging in sizes comparable to grapes and plums. The doctors could not fathom how my husband was for the most part fully functioning, let alone still breathing, with a poisonous mass of that magnitude and aggression invading his body. We were told by multiple physicians that it was a huge miracle in and of itself from the beginning to have even been granted a diagnosis.

Every medical professional that we came in contact with was mind-blown by Cody's case. They couldn't understand why he had *this*. Despite him being born with an underlying health condition, each physician promised it wasn't the cause of this cancer's development. Truly, I couldn't help but notice Cody wasn't like the rest of the cancer patients. He seemed so much younger, healthier, more vibrant, and cheery. His strength, motivation, and uplifting spirits made me feel like his case wasn't *that* severe. Honestly, sometimes I wasn't 100 percent convinced those scans matched my guy. If it wasn't for his physically distended abdomen, I would've been in denial that he had cancer.

We sought out other larger hospitals that had more experience in rare, abnormal cases, but no one other than the Vanderbilt-Ingram Cancer Center in Nashville, Tennessee, could see us soon enough. Other facilities that specialized in this type of cancer were booked months out. COVID-19 wasn't making the application process to get us in sooner any easier, either. We were told not to waste any more time. Cody and I quickly became agitated with the lack of urgency by other hospitals, so after much prayer we decided to make Vanderbilt our home turf. We were racing against the clock and needed treatment and answers immediately. This unknown process and the constant waiting were brutal!

I'll never forget the afternoon we received the phone call explaining the results of his PET scan. He had already been diagnosed, but we were not certain of the cancer's severity or aggression at that point. Cody, some friends, and I were sitting outside on the back porch of our lovely new home, enjoying the beautiful summer day we were blessed with. My husband didn't get far out of my sight in those days, and he was lounging directly to my left. His stoic nature soothed me when not much else would.

As we were all sitting around enjoying one another's company, Cody's cell phone began to ring. At that moment, it felt like time had frozen all around me. I was extremely nervous to hear what the voice on the phone had to say. We had been anticipating this important call for several days. Rambling on and on in her thick foreign accent, the doctor gave us bad news and good news regarding his most recent scan. The bad news was that the cancer was more advanced than they had originally thought. Initially, through the ultrasounds and MRIs, they could see only the invasion in the right hepatic lobe, but this new scan showed that the left hepatic lobe was being compromised, too. The good news was that the cancer was only confined in his liver, and there was no evidence of it spreading beyond that organ despite the enormous size.

As soon as that tough conversation was over, our friends left Cody and me for some privacy to process the new information together. I wanted nothing more than to sink and disappear into my husband's embrace. I longed for his sweet lips to tell me that everything was going to be alright, but the smell of his faint cologne when he pulled me close was just enough to ease the dagger in my chest. His actions spoke louder than any words. The way his body entangled itself into mine, I knew deep down that he was worried about *me*. However, I was distraught for him.

At first, I wasn't exactly sure what to say or think until Cody began to speak. Still holding me tightly, he perched himself onto the ledge near our back door.

Taking my chin in his hands and tilting it up to meet his gaze, he said, "Baby, I view our glass being half-full instead of half-empty. Let's thank God for the good news."

His optimistic outlook over the situation was utterly contagious, and I could see joy and the fire in his eyes. Instantly, I couldn't help but become thankful, too. I grabbed the back of my husband's neck and pressed my forehead against his, closed my eyes, and I began to pray aloud.

God, we want to abundantly thank You for our lives together and for the good news we just received. We want to never stop worshiping You for being faithful and allowing us to still feel so much love. We want to lift up the doctors and nurses who have been and who will be over Cody's care. We pray that they would already know Jesus or that we would show them Jesus along the way. We ask You to continue to shower us with blessings of good news, healing, and strength. And we declare that the enemy be kept away and for You to drown out the ways of this world. Again, no matter what any human tells us, we ask You, Father God, to allow us to focus only on what You say about our situation. We profess that You are the Ultimate Healer, and we are Your precious children. Amen.

To our dismay, Cody could not qualify for a liver transplant. Due to the lesion's massive size, he wasn't able to make the transplant list. According to our oncology team, to qualify for the transplant, there either had to be one single tumor invasion, which that individual tumor had to be smaller than eight centimeters, or in Cody's case—a multiple tumor invasion where none of them could be larger than three centimeters each. According to the American Cancer Society website, the standard was that either one tumor had to be smaller than five centimeters across, or there couldn't be any more than two to three tumors larger than three centimeters. Needless to say, Cody's tumors were exceedingly out of this range.

Without question, I begged and pleaded multiple times for them to find a way to resect my liver as a live donor and give it to him. In my mind, this would have allowed us to avoid the list altogether. When the doctors hesitated, I offered several more times. I wanted to give him my whole darn organ, but these ideas were not realistic. We discussed Cody having a resection of his own liver, a partial hepatectomy, but the cancer had already consumed too much of the organ. The doctors said they wouldn't be able to leave enough liver behind for it to properly function and regenerate itself. Cody and I spoke with the best surgeon at Vanderbilt, and even he wouldn't have touched my love with a ten-foot pole. He promised that any surgeon in their right mind would have told us the exact same thing. Important blood vessels had grown around and through the largest tumor, to the point where any operation or any surgery would not have been safe or successful. He also feared that because of the tumor's size and invasion already, the cancer was in my husband's bloodstream, just merely undetectable at the moment. This would have meant that even if the liver operation were to have been successful, the cancer would have come back or would still be present within his body. To encourage us, he said we would revisit the surgery topic if another treatment option could successfully shrink the tumor. Until then, going under the knife would have been suicide.

This surgeon expressed amazement in Cody's unshakable confidence and matter-of-fact responses to the disappointing news. He expected Cody, like many of his other patients when given upsetting news, to crumble. He was prepared for the waterworks, but the only tears that fell came from me. I had to excuse myself to the restroom a few times during that conversation to flush out all the snot that was building up pressure in my head. My head was internally exploding, and my heart was being shattered all over again. The surgeon and Cody ended up briefly chatting and getting to know one another. He expressed great admiration in my husband's faith and wished us all the luck in the days to come.

Cody's treatment options were limited. He didn't qualify for certain types of radiation or stronger chemo because of their harsh nature. The liver is already an extremely sensitive organ in general, now made even more delicate with the cancer's aggressive attack. Thankfully, our hematology/oncology specialist was excited about the latest immunotherapy treatment with the Bevacizumab (Avastin) and Atezolizumab (Tecentriq) medicines. It seemed promising! With Cody's young age, no major underlying health conditions heightened, his mental stability, and his super-strong body, the medical professionals seemed optimistic that the immunotherapy could work.

All the while, doctors struggled to give us any inkling of a stage or prognosis, because of the rarity of Cody's situation. But eventually, they gave him a 1 percent survival rate that is typically given to all late-stage liver cancer patients. When reviewing scans and analyzing Cody's body, multiple doctors would often express pure amazement in his unbelievable physical strength. Their reactions often overwhelmed me. Yet their responses to how his body was handling the disease also filled me with so much hope that he would live. Those around us felt that if anyone could beat this, it would be him. Despite the survival rate, we felt the odds were in our favor, because God never left our side.

chapter six

Crossing Boundaries

They say the first year of marriage is the toughest, but thankfully that had been a breeze for us. Like I mentioned, Cody and I had a *beautiful* marriage. We had our fair share of disagreements and arguments, but nothing that dangerously divided our home. To be completely honest, those first five weeks after Cody's diagnosis were a complete blur to me. My husband's energy was depleting at an exponential rate. And Cody and I had never been so divided. However, the first five weeks after diagnosis alone were hands down the roughest times in our marriage and not because of the cancer elephant in the room. During this duration period, my mother-in-law had been staying with us.

Since childhood, I had always dreamed of someday having a close relationship with my in-laws, but specifically my future mother-in-law. Always having been a people pleaser, the thought of having a rocky relationship with her devastated me, but the idea of having a close bond with the mother of my mate warmed my heart. I dreamed of being someone she would be proud of for her son to spend the rest of his life with. I longed for a close family dynamic and chemistry for the sake of not only me but for my future husband, our future children, and the generations to come.

Before my husband was diagnosed, I would have considered me and his mom to be fairly close. Not as close as I would've liked, but I had assumed it was due to the distance. We would spend hours at a time on the phone with one other and travel to and from Kentucky to Florida for visits. She told me multiple times throughout our relationship that I was everything she had ever prayed about for her son, and I took great heart to these compliments. She always seemed to be bragging and boasting about me, and in return, I cherished her, too. Many people complimented us on having similar characteristics, and that meant a lot to me at the time. To my knowledge, our relationship was going great previously. She was someone I looked up to, and I adored her.

Unfortunately, her staying with us for five weeks created an unhealthy wedge between the three of us. There are two sides to every story, but to me, I wished she had stepped up more to help with Cody without being asked. Mind you that I am fully aware that I have a rather high-strung personality, and I have a hard time sitting still. This has made it difficult for me to ask others for help—it eats me alive sometimes when others take what I perceive to be my load. Cody warned me rather early on that she might mistake my independence and feel unneeded. He forewarned me that she could overstep and outspeak. He encouraged me to include her with chores around the house more, but I was so invested and one-track-minded on him, that I didn't feel the need to go out of my way to entertain or make a to-do list for her. She was family so I expected her to understand and to hop in where she felt led. We often miscommunicated.

To put it briefly, while none of us had bad intentions, Cody and I had not set proper boundaries from the start. This was our home, our marriage, our decisions, and our life. We blamed her, and she blamed me. Poor Cody was smushed in the middle and forced to play peacekeeper, when in reality this volatile time should have been all about him. Outsiders soon began to feel and see the tension building up inside of our home.

I had an inkling that things would get distorted within the first seventy-two hours upon her arrival.

On this day, my mother-in-law and I were in the kitchen packing up boxes together for our move, Cody was in the living room lying down on the couch, and we were all making the best out of the day we were given. Cody's mentor had briefly stopped in to deliver us lunch, and we were all grateful to be sharing another meal.

Suddenly, Cody rushed to the bathroom where he started throwing up. I instinctively took my place beside him, making sure he wasn't alone. We had developed a system for these episodes. I would hand him toilet paper to wipe his mouth and to plug his nosebleeds that followed, and I would then watch for anything unusual to come up, like I had always done and been instructed to by the doctors.

Now, this was his mom's first time witnessing this. She took her place behind him, rubbing his back, repeating "Jesus" over and over again. At first, I remember thinking that Cody was in good hands, and I felt blessed to have her there with us. I felt confident that we weren't going to leave his side for a single second. While he was heaving this time, speckles of blood began to come up. I instantly went into Nurse Jackie mode, remembering what the doctors had told me. They warned me that the liver was such a sensitive organ and to keep a close eye out for vomiting or coughing up any blood in the days to come.

Their instructions were clear as day to me: "Take him to the emergency room if you notice anything like this. It could mean internal bleeding."

Once he was finished and back on the couch, I called his doctors to confirm what I should do. Bring him in?

Their response was, "Yes, immediately. We will have a room waiting for him."

As soon as this was communicated, I dashed upstairs to throw his medicine, a fresh shirt, phone chargers, and whatever else into a bag. But once I came downstairs, I found Cody and his mom still sitting on the couch where I had left them. He was supposed to have already been making his way to the car. Cody was showing resistance to going, but that wasn't unusual behavior for him, because he hated going to the doctor. Hopeful, I glanced over at his mom for help. I thought as a mother she would have her son's health in mind, too.

To my surprise, she began to vouch for him, stating that he did not want to go to the emergency room and that going was not necessary over such little blood. She assured me that if the blood progressed in the next couple of hours, he would go, but right now I was being unreasonable. I stood there for a few moments like a statue in complete disbelief that she was telling me this. Last I checked, she didn't have her MD license, let alone been to any appointments with her son to hear what the doctors were saying about his condition. As a wife, I was incredibly cautious and attentive to my husband's every symptom because of the mad love I have for him and the education I was experiencing with him now daily.

Ultimately, we ended up not going to the hospital. But thankfully, thankfully, thankfully there was no more blood that came up on that day. It is what it is now, but what if there had been? What if Cody had been experiencing internal bleeding somewhere? What if, what if, what if? My heart was shattered at the what if's that his mom could not see. Of course he didn't want to go to the doctor. This man despised going to the doctor, but I had learned as a caregiver that sometimes you have to push the patient. Without my persistence in him going to the doctor in the first place to get checked out, I'm not sure we would've caught the cancer when we did.

This situation was just one of the *many* unfortunate circumstances that made our relationships and this time so incredibly hard. Although this particular situation did not resort in immediate conflict, it opened a door for that wedge to be set. This later would result in his mom bad-mouthing me to him and other family members behind my back, causing me to become extremely defensive and standoffish. She would interrupt our personal marriage decisions and discussions with her own unwarranted input, which would lead to her own guilt for abandoning her son in his darkest season.

Honestly, I didn't know if writing about certain dramas we faced during our journey would be the best idea. But if speaking the full and vulnerable truth helps at least one person, then let God use me as His vessel. Jesus teaches in Mark 10:9, "Therefore what God has joined together, let no one separate." I have found that when striving to serve the Lord during an ultimate test, Satan will still attempt to break you in the most surprising of ways. Boundaries were paramount even towards our dearest loved ones. We sought to show grace in protecting not only our sacred space, but also our marriage that God ordained.

chapter seven

Back in the Game

Meanwhile, we remained in straight survival mode despite the constant bickering within our household. The immunotherapy combined with our lifestyle changes had been working wonderfully at first. His tumor markers were steadily decreasing after his first round of treatment. However, during round two of treatment, his liver had a negative reaction to the drugs. This reaction caused his liver to significantly swell, along with several horrible side effects. My husband looked to be seven months pregnant from the inflammation going on internally in his abdomen. Our medical team suggested we pause all treatment temporarily in hopes that Cody's body would naturally recover.

My daily routine was pure madness on top of it all. And for a while, it was self-inflicted. We had people who were willing to help with anything and everything that we needed, but Cody and I were often too stubborn to reach out and ask for help. Without the help of my colleagues, my mom, and our closest friends, there is no way I would've made it through. While 24/7 tending to my husband's every need, I focused on my rather successful real estate business during his naps, TV time, or in the middle of the night if there was stillness in Cody's condition.

There were many nights where neither working nor sleeping was an option due to my mind racing and heart aching. Often, I felt completely worthless in helping heal my husband. Half of the time, I would just restlessly lie awake. And sometimes I would notice he wasn't beside me in our bed or in his recliner but lying on the ground. So some nights were spent sleeping on the uncomfortable floor beside him, making sure he never felt alone. Perhaps our furniture wasn't doing the trick in providing comfort, yet he never complained too much.

At the beginning of July, Cody and I moved into our first house, with the help of several dear friends who completely took over as our moving crew. So not only was I steadily unpacking boxes, but I was now trying to keep a 3,000+ square foot home clean, too. Grocery store runs, running errands left and right, taking all of the phone calls to update our family and friends, learning how to cook healthier dishes for his diet, preparing these new delights, taking him to and from every doctor appointment and treatments, being cautious not to bring home COVID-19, juggling the passive-aggressive wrath of some of my in-laws, and trying to balance my own personal needs. This was only a sliver of the chaos. I say all of this to document that it was extremely *overwhelming*. However, I loved nothing more than to take these pressures off of my husband so that he could solely focus on his healing. As much as I wanted to take his disease as my own, if I couldn't do that, the least I could do was take the controllable pressures away from him.

At the end of July, Cody's mom went back home to Florida, and we were able to process and work through our new normal. Things were beginning to calm down under the Eubanks' roof. Although the tension between me and my mate had gotten tremendously better since she left, there was still unexplained stress lingering. I was now wired to be his immediate care-taker instead of his loving, comforting wife. Our conversations solely revolved around his health. I viewed him as fragile, and he viewed me as a second mom when he really needed his wife. I missed him, and I am certain that he missed me, too. What was missing? What were we doing wrong?

On August 11, 2020, in particular, we noticed the game change for the better. I felt extremely hopeful that Cody and I would recover from the brief season that had gotten us off-balanced. We needed supportive encouragement, loving criticism, and renewed confidence. I remember the impact this day had on us and even confided the sequence of events to several close friends afterwards.

On that sunny Tuesday afternoon, a few of Cody's former flag football buddies came over to present him with their five-foot-tall, championship-winning trophy. They had dedicated themselves to winning the game for him and in his honor. The trophy was their healing token towards their brother. This gesture was beautiful.

I invited a girlfriend over for a casual drink and girl time, while the guys hung out and did their thing. Cody definitely needed his boys, and I totally needed my gal. Shelby and I had actually met through Cody. Cody and her boyfriend, Jeryn, used to play on the same flag football team when Cody and I first started going steady. Over the course of a few games, naturally Shelby and I became great friends. She understood me to the core and would soon become one of my closest friends, resulting in her standing beside us as a bridesmaid on our most monumental day. She was exactly whom I needed at the time, because I unleashed the beast and vented to her about the recent stresses of life. She certainly got an earful from me that day during one of our earlier conversations. I had totally snapped!

Once she was able to help calm me down, she escorted me inside where the guys were gathered around our dining room table. She took a seat at the head of the table, and I took a seat next to my Cody. Two unfamiliar faces were seated around the table with us aside from Jeryn. Let's call them Bob and Aaron.

After a friendly introduction, Aaron, who was seated at the opposite head of the table, began to speak. He was a bit hesitant at first, but he confessed that he was a cancer survivor. He said he prayed about opening up and revealing his past to us on his drive over to our house. He ultimately felt led by God to share his testimony with us. This wasn't something he went out broadcasting to the world, so it was nice he remained obedient and humbled himself before Christ. I was immediately intrigued and had many questions for him. His openness and honesty inspired me and my husband. When our conversation was concluding, Aaron led a powerful prayer for Cody's strength and continued healing. *Amen!*

Afterwards, Bob had to leave, but Aaron stuck around. Cody, Shelby, and I engaged in conversation until it was time for his herbs and medicine. When I entered the master bathroom to collect his herbal supplements, I found Jeryn and Aaron lingering in deep discussion in front of Cody's bathroom mirror.

Earlier in July, I had taken my husband to a local iridologist. Iridology is an alternative medicine technique whose proponents claim that patterns, colors, and other characteristics of the iris can be examined to determine information about a patient's systemic health. This was completely foreign to us, but anything was worth a shot. We were willing to do whatever it took to ensure that Cody beat this cancer and had the best chance for survival. This iridologist was also an avid herbalist.

He was confident that specific herbs and proper nutrition would help Cody's body fight considerably.

Needless to say, after that beneficial iridology appointment concluded, this excessively crazy wife recruited two of her health-nut friends to completely empty out our fridge, pantries, and deep freezers and restock them with all fresh, organic foods. Nothing processed, fried, injected, or sugar-filled was found in our residence. Sure, I got super mocked for it, but I was only doing what was best for Cody's health.

On my husband's bathroom mirror was a chart that I handmade for him. It consisted of his herbal schedule. It elaborated on what times to take which herbs, how much of which herbs to take when, along with what each herb was doing for his body. There was a motivational saying and fitting Bible verse on each page, too. Everything was perfectly color coded. I didn't want us to miss *anything*.

When I walked in the bathroom, Aaron was staring at the chart in wild disbelief.

"Did you do *this*?" he asked in awe.

It was truly no big deal. I certainly didn't think a stranger would be standing in my restroom analyzing four sheets of paper, but he was floored by it. It felt good for my soul to have been acknowledged for this simple act.

After gathering up Cody's handful of herbs, we rejoined him and Shelby in the dining room. Upon entering the room, Aaron was the first to speak.

He lovingly scolded Cody by saying, "Bro, do you have any idea how much I would've loved and benefitted from this kind of support during my cancer journey? You have an amazing wife.

She's not only walking beside you in this; she is in the trenches fighting this battle with you."

My heart instantly stopped. He was right. I quickly glanced over to look at my husband, not sure how he was going to appreciate those comments coming from another man whom we weren't exactly close with. But Cody smiled.

"I know," he said while confidently looking at me. "She is the best and has not missed a beat!"

That salute felt great. I needed that compliment from someone entirely disconnected from our lives. For someone to observe something so small and feel its power was huge! Cody needed to hear it, too. We both had been slacking in the encouragement department lately and needed to be brought back to square one. We noticeably felt our fire heat back up in the days to come, and this resulted in our love for one another growing stronger than ever before.

chapter eight

Facing the Public

Roughly two months after Cody's diagnosis, we decided to let the Facebook world know about his health and our challenges. Our close family, friends, and people who'd heard through the grapevine knew, but so many people had no clue what we were facing. My husband's wish was to not draw attention or spotlight our family. However, I wanted as many prayers going up to the Ultimate Healer as possible. Some may remember this post from August 18, 2020, that we drafted up together:

> Despite the global circumstances, 2020 had been great to us thus far. Celebrating our first wedding anniversary, both businesses booming, attempting to grow our family, and our first house. Our life got flipped upside down on June 15, 2020. My husband was diagnosed with cancer. My Cody. My Love. My World. Diagnosed with the c-word. *cringe*

When the doctors told us there was a tumor the size of a large cantaloupe or small watermelon with other "smaller" tumors the size of grapes and plums invading my husband's holy temple, my heart sunk and shattered into 10 billion pieces. It just doesn't make sense. Why us? Why my Cody? Here's why—because my Cody is anointed by God Almighty to win this victory and glorify Him while doing it and beyond. He is and will be an example for generations to come that the God we serve is a mountain moving God that never ceases to fail.

These past few months have been some of the worst yet best moments of our lives. Our faith and trust in God has exceeded what we ever thought possible. He reveals himself to us DAILY in ways we may not have seen before. We're learning to determine what's truly important in life. We adore & appreciate the family & friends who intentionally pray for us, radiate & share positivity with us, and that have gone above & beyond for our comfort and needs during this season. Blessings from God come in ALL different shapes, sizes, and colors.

Those who have chosen to make Cody's health about them and have used this delicate time as an excuse to stir drama or divide us—shame on you. How pitiful and downright disrespectful. The enemy comes to steal, kill, and destroy, and unfortunately he is using people we never would've imagined. The only thing that should matter is his healing not the opinions, thoughts, or concerns of anyone else for that matter. We simply don't have the strength or energy to feed negativity, definitely not now—but ever. Don't let Satan use you as a pawn in this game of his. We love you and we forgive you.

One week from tomorrow we will go in for Cody's 3rd round of treatment. The nurses, doctors, and staff at Vanderbilt in Nashville have been incredible. I cannot thank them enough for loving on my Cody! Cody is a superstar & stronger than we all imagined (those of you who know him know that he's nothing shy of amazing all around). I am HONORED to be his wife. Hills & valleys, you'll find me at his flank.

Cody is healed in the spiritual realm—we believe this. Jesus paid the price and thought of Cody when he took his last human breath on the cross. The power of prayer is ALIVE & REAL!

Please send all your love & positive vibes while keeping our family in your thoughts & prayers. We truly do feel each prayer vibrantly.

—Cody & Jackie

The amount of love and support that came from our community was overwhelming in the most beautiful of ways. We felt beyond loved. Several friend groups set up meal trains that helped out tremendously. Gift cards for groceries and restaurants during our travels were provided by countless friends. Cards, posters, paintings, kind texts, and gift baskets filled with love brought many smiles to our faces. We were put on several prayer chains, and it totally felt like the whole city was praying for his recovery and our peace. Some people even got creative by donating to charities on our behalf that Cody and I were passionate about. A few friends even designed and sold black wristbands with white lettering that said, "#CodyCrushesCancer" on them. My favorite was seeing the many smiles these wristbands brought to Cody's face when seeing people out in public wearing them.

Cody and I had a husband-and-wife duo who served as our mentors. They played a special role in keeping us grounded in our faith and in our marriage. They were always there for advice regarding our finances, and they assisted in helping us navigate through the medical system. They were the only ones besides me that Cody allowed to attend his doctors' appointments. Their willingness to go above and beyond was comforting to know that we weren't ever alone.

Each simple yet monumental act of kindness empowered us to realize that better days were coming, and God had our back no matter what. We truly couldn't thank everyone enough. Our gratefulness will forever be there.

chapter nine

My Connection with Christ

Although Cody was an important man in my life, I would like to use this chapter to let you in on the sacredness of someone else. Someone who's been pursuing my soul for what feels like light years now. He knows me far better than I will ever know myself, and He had sought me out long before I accepted Him to be worthy. He has always and will forever hold the number one spot in my heart. Jesus.

I love Jesus! In fact, I'm smiling ear to ear writing this because Christ and I have a *very* intimate relationship. My relationship with Him started with my parents. They are fantastic people who love the Lord, too, so they were the ones to introduce me. When I was around middle-school age, my mom orchestrated the youth group nights and events, while my dad played a more behind-the-scenes role with kid transport and cleanup. They loved hosting not only the youth, but everyone in our home, and they were devoted to loving all of God's children. To this day, they are as selfless as it comes. If one of our family members or friends is in need, my parents go out of their way to extend a helping hand with whatever the need may be. Growing up, we always prayed before meals, before bed, sang catchy Bible songs like *Jesus Loves Me* in our spare time, and almost never missed Sunday church.

My parents taught me and my four siblings to love others as Christ loves us. They educated us on the doctrine, and they strived to keep Jesus in the midst of our family. As a reflection of their parenting and way of life, I accepted Jesus Christ as my Lord and Savior in the eighth grade while away at church camp with some friends shortly after moving to Kentucky. However, I still longed for a deeper relationship with Christ.

In the fall of 2016, I was working first shift at Planet Fitness as the girl wearing purple behind the front desk. I love my former colleagues. I love each gym member. And I loved that job. For a while, every morning at 6:00 a.m. (more like 6:15 a.m. because your girl was always running late), I would sit with my colleagues, Courtney Dalcourt and Luther Salyers, and an occasional gym member or two at the front desk for hours at a time and discuss His Holy Word. They helped challenge my way of thinking and my feelings about how I viewed this life, the universe, and eternity. Our conversations, debates, and studies often got *deep*. I began to *desperately*, like the desert searching for rain, long to become closer to the Maker of heaven.

I'll never forget how Courtney encouraged me to get my own paper copy of the Holy Bible instead of using the Bible mobile app. He warned me of the enemy's sly distractions of sending text messages, prompting Facebook notifications, or receiving a phone call in the midst of spending time in the Word when using a mobile device. I knew the enemy was lurking, but the ways in which he would be attacking was alarming to me.

After a while I became more and more confident in incorporating biblical principles and spending time with Jesus into my everyday life. As time passed, His Spirit revealed to me that His reign cannot be confined into a box. My faith in these new discoveries began to trump my own personal feelings, because it became evident that I serve the one, true, and only God that will never fail me. Around this time is when I started to truly grasp the simplicity of religion, too. He is so much larger than my tiny flesh can possibly comprehend while on this earth. However, I began to apply what I was learning about Him, not only in between the four walls of the gym, but with the rest of the world.

One day, Courtney came to work, rambling on and on about the night he had just had with a group of Christian believers. Honestly, he freaked me out when he mentioned how they gathered together in someone's living room, fellowshipped for a while, then shut off the lights, and started praising God in the pitch dark. *O-kay* . . . then he invited me to join them; but even with all the trust I had for him, I was skeptical of this unknown. He kept attending this gathering weekly, and I couldn't help but notice that each week his enthusiasm and passion for Christ overflowed. I was insanely curious, yet reluctant to attend for a couple of months. I kid you not, I thought it was a cult.

On October 23, 2016, my life changed forever. I took him up on the offer to attend what this group of people, broken sinners just like you and me, referred to themselves as Freedom. I had no clue what to expect when I pulled into the driveway of an average, middle-class-looking home. For some reason, I expected to gather at an ordinary church building, but I was quickly reminded of Matthew 18:20: "For where two or more are gathered in my name, there am I among them." Church can be anywhere we call upon Him.

When I entered through the threshold, I was greeted by smiling faces of fellow believers. I admit, I was nervous. With my red flags all the way up and my tail tingling to approach with caution, that night went nothing how I had expected. The host lowered the lights to where we were standing in the dark, and we began to worship. Some bodies were up moving, while others were sitting still. Some voices were singing, while others sat in silence. Some people were reading verses out of the Bible, while others were preaching from memory. This time was designed to praise Him however one felt led by His Spirit. This time was intentionally sectioned off each week from our busy lives to solely focus on praising Him. No barriers, no distractions, no pressure, just you and Him.

That night His Spirit lovingly paralyzed me from head to toe to where I could only focus on His majesty. This stillness with Him was unlike anything He had ever allowed me to witness. What He was manifesting to me built up a burning desire in my soul to *crave* a personal, intimate relationship with the Trinity *in Him being one remarkable, fascinating unit.* As I sat on the corner of a stranger's comfy sectional sofa, it felt like in that moment time was then frozen as God Almighty took me to a place with Him so much deeper than I had ever experienced before. No words could possibly express the night I had dancing with my King, the Lord of eternity. My body was elsewhere with Him experiencing ultimate peace and goodness. He revealed how temporary everything around me is, and He showed me the big picture of His reign. He fought for my soul, and it was divulged to me. He had proven Himself vastly to me, and in return I vowed that He had won over my loyalty for life. I wanted more of His presence; I want more of Him *still!*

For the next several months, every Monday night I continued to attend Freedom to go dancing in the dark in the arms of my Savior. Growing more and more comfortable and confident in who He says I am, my desire for worldly pleasure and gain grew less and less. My tolerance for energy that displeased God grew thin. Although the dark-dancing nights with my Freedom friends began to fade due to life, of course, I am forever thankful for that initial season with Christ, who showed me to seek Him in creative ways. Every time I close my eyes, His kingdom *purple* intensely follows me while pursuing me vigorously. I can find Him anywhere, because He is always present. He is in *all* things. He is in *everything.*

Jesus put this prayer on my heart then, and it is my continuous prayer today: "God, when people see me, allow Yourself to shine through. Allow Your love and goodness to exude out of me. Make me more like Jesus for the glory of Your kingdom. Use me, God, like only You can!" My favorite praise is "Thank you God for pursuing my soul endlessly. Thank you for putting a desire in my heart to want to know You. Thank you for choosing me to be Your daughter."

Now, He knows how to get my attention like no other. His charm is captivating and unrestricted. I get smitten by His gentle, tender love and His ability to spank my bottom when I've been too naughty. He keeps it real with me and allows His Holy Ghost to convict my heart when I walk out of line. He is always there to listen to me, even when I do not have the words to speak. His presence knows how to take my breath away and give it right back in full-fledged power. When I am weak, He gives me His unending strength. He is my Ultimate Defender and in whom I seek refuge and shelter. He has fought battles on my behalf again and again and again. He is *always* there for me like a knight in shining armor rescuing His princess from the wickedness of this world. Even though His love is incomprehensible at times, He immensely drowns me in the truest form of love. He will always be the anchor for my soul, ruler of my heart, and has the number-one seat as my absolute one true love.

Does my bond with the Lord make me more holy or superior to others? Absolutely not! I am not angelic by any means. Until He calls me home to heaven, I am still only human. I have much to work on within myself and definitely fall short of the glory of God, daily. I am a ruthless, dirty sinner. Unfortunately, I have a mouth like a sailor sometimes, and I've missed Sunday church more times than I can count. I am more stubborn than a mule, I have enjoyed sex out of wedlock way too much, and I can be overly outspoken when asked for my opinion on a topic. My patience runs thin at times, I enjoy listening to "feel good" music of every genre, I have lied on more than one occasion, I have said and done things I've regretted, and I often have a really, really good time with my friend tequila.

I assume the worst sometimes, overthink much too often, and sometimes I fear and dwell on the tiniest of problems, therefore relinquishing control from the Throne. Yes, I am a control freak. I love my piercings and my tattoos, and I ignore the speed limit signs, too. I can be selfish, I often act and speak on emotion, I have partaken and probably will partake in my fair share of pointless gossip, and I am the worst enabler to those who need to seek Him out in their own lives. I am a huge Christian hypocrite. I've judged the judgmental, and often should take my own advice that I give to others. This list runs miles deep and unfortunately will until I am in heaven with my Maker, but my actions are between me and my Father, for it is unfair for one sinner to cast stones at another. I have received His undeserving mercy, time and time again. He displays His perfect peace and patience with this strong-willed daughter of His daily. Needless to say, I am not perfect and will never claim to be. If it were left in my hands, I would fail every single time.

> Lord, I am beyond thankful for Your mercy and grace
> in my life, and for sending Your son, Jesus Christ, to
> wash all my sin away. You command the sun to rise and to set.
> You know the exact number of the hairs on my head. You have
> the power to open my eyes each morning, and You hold the
> foresight to know my very next move. I feel Your hugs in the
> wind, and I see Your love in the eyes of innocent newborns.
> I am thankful that You want me despite my flaws and
> shortcomings. I surrender all that I am for Your cause, for
> I am nothing without You. Amen.

A friend has shared the following story with me a few times now, and I feel compelled to share it here. One day, she had a conversation with her son-in-law who did not desire to have a relationship with the Lord. He was a very kind man but confused about his purpose in life. One day, he bluntly asked her, "So you believe the God of the Universe knows you personally and actually talks to you?" Without hesitation, she replied, "Yes!" He mocked and laughed at her hysterically, saying, "That is the most arrogant thing I've ever heard." She said, "Well, it would be arrogant if I believed I was the only one He speaks to, but I believe anyone can have this relationship with Him." Her response was priceless. This is the truth and so very powerful. Our God makes Himself available to anyone who calls upon His name!

On March 20, 2017, Christ made His instructions for my life known to me. Someone at Freedom received a vision from above about me. They felt a strong urge to inform me that the Lord wanted to bless me with something, but there was a veil in my path that needed to be torn in order to reach the treasure on the other side. Immediately, I knew exactly what this meant.

After much prayer for confirmation, two nights later I broke up with my high school sweetheart of nearly four good years to embrace the unknown. Again, I will never understand the timing of God, but I won't doubt Him. It was nothing short of divine intervention that the very next day I met my Cody.

chapter ten

The Awkward Hug

The evening of April 18, 2017, will forever be an event in time that Cody and I could never quite agree on. His perception and mine on how this sequence of events went down were two totally different realities. I have laughed many times writing and reliving this chapter. So here it goes.

In my defense, I remember being exhausted on this day in particular from working a double shift at Planet Fitness and not getting good, quality sleep. At the time, I was still taking online college courses through Western Kentucky University's dual enrollment program. Since pursuing my track and field dream was no longer an option, drowning myself in a job I enjoyed became how I chose to spend the majority of my time. As a result, college had been slowly shrinking on my priority list, so the only time I put towards my assignments and education was during the middle of the night. Undoubtedly, I was probably slap-happy and delusional by the time nightfall rolled around.

It was a muggy, dewy Tuesday evening on the track. The misty breeze was faint and cool. The stadium lights lit up the entire vicinity in the dark of the night. Track season for our athletes was still in full swing. The season for both of our teams was going great thus far. A couple of Cody's athletes were breaking new school records, and mine were thriving, too.

Since our initial encounter, Cody and I had each been keeping tabs on the other's athletes. We would speak accordingly here and there when we would see one another at the meets. Admittedly, I did enjoy his company around the track. He didn't view or treat me as a former South Warren competitor, unlike some of the other, older coaches who had watched me grow up and compete locally throughout the years. He viewed me as a current coach and respected my authority and knowledge of the sport. He was without a doubt a nice, attractive guy, and he was easy to discuss the events and sport with, but in no way was I interested in him like *that*.

As the meet was coming to an end, Cody, another coach (Franklin Simpson's head coach at the time), one of their young female athletes, that athlete's mom, and I were all huddled together having an uplifting conversation about this athlete's skillset and future. She had really taken to me, so Cody thought that if I gave her a few encouraging words, it would be helpful and enlightening. Everyone was in awe of the special talent this young lady possessed, and we believed that she wasn't even scratching the surface of her full potential. Her ability to keep up with and beat other athletes who had been competing for years before her was very impressive. She was going to be phenomenal if she stuck with her training.

When the conversation concluded, Cody was the first one to break away from the huddle. He casually made his way around the circle with handshakes, goodbyes, and a "good job" to the racer. When he got around to telling me goodbye, I confidently bear-hugged the snot out of him! At the moment, it felt like instinct. However, he immediately threw his hands in the air in shock, for this probably wasn't an appropriate setting. We barely knew one another, and I hadn't given him even a small, subtle side hug. This was a swaddle-like-I've-known-you-forever hug! I instantly became embarrassed when I realized how this came across. *Oh my goodness. My, oh my. What have I done?*

"Are we giving out hugs now, coach?!" he yelled, while frantically looking over at the other coach and parent with his hands still reaching for the sky.

The embarrassment I felt was inevitable, but what really kicked was not knowing what in the world possessed me to hang on for as long as I did. I felt humiliated and didn't know what to say or do next. He was probably mortified, too.

Now, let me elaborate and explain this scene further. Those who know me know I can be a rather affectionate, loving person. I am an extreme extrovert with no sense of boundaries for human space at times. Did I mention how exhausted I was, too? When Cody swung around towards my direction, he raised his left arm in the air while dangling his keys to avoid elbowing me in the face. Naturally, I was perched at his flank and right there in hug-territory, where I had assumed he meant to be. My friendliness was harshly mistaken by the male species, yet again. Welcome to my life.

However, if you were to ask him his side of the story, he would say that he hadn't raised his arm to hug. He would say he was merely readjusting his duffle bag up onto his shoulder and had no clue I was right there behind him. He preached that I wanted him and couldn't help myself but to embrace him with a gigantic hug. And that I was desperate to have him. He would go on and on about how I had been lurking in the shadows waiting for my chance to swipe him up. *Okay, buddy!* For some strange reason, his charming self always convinced people that this was the true version of the story of how we began our journey together. His enthusiasm was priceless to witness, watching him retell this story, and he always brought me to my knees in laughter. This guy was something else!

The next morning, I woke up to find a new friend request on Facebook along with a private message. It was him! I was extremely resistant to accept and reply. How I'd made a fool of myself in front of him and others was not at the top of my agenda to discuss for the day. Clearly, I was still unsettled by that episode—not my finest moment, indeed. Yet after a few hours, I built up the courage to rip off the Band-Aid to accept his friend request and message him back.

Cody: "Hey coach! I was able to snoop on your page and check out your recent endeavors. Good job and congrats! . . . and btw I hope I didn't make you feel weird or anything like that last night. I just wasn't expecting a hug. Much appreciated, just wasn't expecting it lol"

Jackie: "What's up? Thank you so much. Gosh . . . I am so embarrassed! I totally thought you were the one coming in for a hug! I am so sorry. Hahaha"

Cody: "As for the hug don't be embarrassed nor apologize. It did look like you were waiting on it because you were ready lol. Or maybe you read my mind?? Nonetheless, it's now a standard at this point. So if you are single, I'm expecting my hug ma'am."

To this day, I will never delete those initial conversations. *Effortlessly*, I confirmed being single, and instantly asked about his relationship with the Lord. We messaged about our faith in Jesus Christ and how blessed we both were in those particular seasons of our lives. We bounced back and forth for a bit until he boldly sparked the question.

Cody: "Would you like to grab coffee sometime? That's if you drink coffee."

It tickled me that he added that last sentence. I certainly did not drink coffee. Unless he wanted to witness the Energizer bunny on crack and the coffee scent sweating out of my pores, it was best that we did something else. And something else we did indeed.

A couple of days later, I met him at his apartment. We drove together down to Franklin, Kentucky, where he took me out to his buddy's farm. This friend had recently been in a horrible car accident. Praise Jesus for his full and complete healing, but during his recovery, Cody was voluntarily helping tend to his animals and yard work. Right away, he put my butt to work! He later joked that I was under a strict interview process, and he was merely testing to see if I would be weeded out. Heavy lifting, sweating bullets, and stepping in feces was only a fraction of the fun we had on that long afternoon. Without even truly knowing me or me him, he was already speaking to my inner tomboy. My daddy didn't raise a preppy girl. To me, it was a glamorous first date!

Afterwards, once all the animals were properly taken care of, he took me down the road to his grandma's house for another exciting adventure. When we pulled into the driveway, his grandmother and one of his aunts were sitting on the front porch like they were waiting on us. I could have felt their stares of curiosity from a mile away. Instantly, I started blushing. My nervousness was inescapable. I was in no way ready or presentable to meet his family, especially not on our first date. We took forever to get out of his car because I was not mentally prepared for this surprise! Nor was I dressed appropriately from being on the farm all afternoon. After Cody did some convincing and gave me much reassurance, I took a deep breath and got out of the car.

His grandma and aunt smiled ear to ear when I stepped onto the porch. They seemed to be equally as surprised to meet me. They were very welcoming and inquisitive towards me, and I later learned why they seemed giggly over my presence. Cody was not one to bring women home or around his family, so the news of him bringing me there cycled throughout the family rapidly.

Once we got our hellos and goodbyes out of the way, Cody and I walked around the house to the spacious backyard where he fired up his four-wheeler. I had always loved four-wheelers but hadn't ridden one in years. I was beyond excited! Hopping on the back and wrapping my arms around him for safety, we drove it up, down, and around hills for countless hours until sunset.

Cody was a manly man, and I couldn't have been more impressed. His appreciation for the great outdoors was obvious. He wasn't afraid to get down and dirty to accomplish our chores at the farm nor did he care for us to get a bit messy during our four-wheeler ride, and I was very attracted by those attributes. His respect towards not only me, but to the other women in his life spoke volumes. He used his manners like "yes, ma'am" and "excuse me," held the doors open for us, and held the car door open for me while getting in and out. Our conversations weren't surface level—they were raw and deep. Plus, I was a sucker for his love for Christ. I definitely wanted to see him again.

Since he had set up such an amazing first date, I was in charge of scheduling our second one. I asked him to come to church with me, where a mutual friend of ours would be preaching that upcoming Sunday. We were both excited to be in attendance and had been inseparable since. We could tell this was going to be the start of a beautiful, lifelong relationship.

chapter eleven

Walking on Water

Our relationship wasn't always easy. At first, many people weren't too accepting of me and Cody as a couple. With a thirteen-year age difference, several of our close peers and family members couldn't understand how our dynamic would work. In the very beginning, I was only twenty years old, recently out of a long-term relationship, and couldn't even have a legal drink yet. Certain individuals thought he was robbing me of my youth and stealing my innocence. This brought out many ignorant comments, such as how he was grooming and preying on me. People didn't take time to get to know us as a couple. Instead, rumors were spread about me chasing him for money and being young, dumb, and naïve. If only they knew what we knew or saw what we could see all along.

On another note, we kept a close group of friends who uncondi-tionally adored us together. They didn't see our ages as an issue, but as a beautiful union of two individuals madly in love. They were there to support us during the good times and bad, and they offered help and guidance with whatever we needed to grow our bond. Cody was very intentional about being selective of the company we kept. He was always protecting us from the external, negative forces that were of the world and not coming from the Lord.

I thought I loved and knew Christ well before meeting Cody. But he loved Jesus just as much, if not more than me! As a result, during the course of our relationship, my thirst for Jesus grew abundantly. It was so beautiful to me how Cody's go-to was to dive into the Word to feel closer to Christ, while mine was to blast worship music and sing praises to seek that connection. Together, we were able to blend the two approaches for a healthy balance to keep growing in Him. We realized that spending time in the Word and engaging in conversation with Him are equally as important. Now which is more important: breathing in or breathing out?

Cody was notorious for saying to me, "I've got you and God has got us." As the chosen spiritual leader of our household, anytime he would say this, my heart would skip a beat.

Women, there is nothing, absolutely nothing, more attractive than a man who fears God! And men, the Lord will prosper you and take you farther than your wildest dreams if you truly humble yourself and sacrifice your family before Him. Reference

Genesis 22. It's about the story of Abraham and how he was willing to lead his only son, Isaac, to the mountaintop. He was fully prepared to sacrifice his boy in obedience to his Master. Suddenly at the last minute, God supplied a ram as an offering instead of the young boy. Jehovah Jireh will provide for you and bless you for your submission towards Him.

One has to understand that in a relationship, the balance may not always be 50/50. Sometimes one partner may dip and the other will have to pick up their mate accordingly. That scale may be 60/40 or even 30/70 at times. Cody and I had often encouraged one another to never stop leaning on God. He was our way of balancing back out, and He did this through the other one's support. If God was for us, the troubles and tribulations we were facing had to disappear. And if those trying times didn't disappear in our fleshly existence, there must have been a reason He was bringing us through that current storm. Perhaps there was a promised land on the other side, and we simply needed to trust that His plan was good. After every storm, He gives a rainbow to signify His promises for good to His people. All we needed to remember was Psalm 46:10: "Be still and know that I am God." We were chosen for God's team, and He is the only player we needed on our side to win the game.

As cliché as it sounds, the cancer journey that was to come furthered our desire to lean on our heavenly Father yet again. It's a love and trust that seems limitless. It felt like God never stopped showering us with love during our entire journey. The amount of love and support that came from our community was overwhelming in the most beautiful of ways. We felt beyond loved.

I'll always cherish the times strangers near and far felt led to reach out with warm wishes, prayers for our strength and healing, and towards the end—their admiration and condolences. They said our story was inspiring and inspirational to them, but the impact they made on me and Cody was undeniable. Without a shadow of a doubt, God was using their obedience in sending words of encouragement in those dark moments to keep Himself alive inside of us. The validation He was pouring in our direction gave us confirmation to press on. Right when we thought we couldn't possibly dive any deeper into Him, He pulled us even closer through love that flowed in various ways. We knew we couldn't make it through this season without Him. We needed to be in sync with whatever He had planned even if our hearts would be broken.

Cody and I had many conversations about this topic throughout the years.

"How do people not see God in all things? Why can't people worship Him not only in the good times but during the bad seasons, too? Why can't they praise Him in the midst of a storm?"

We often asked these questions to one another. We would have tunnel vision and not be able to comprehend how people didn't *get it*. It wasn't until my love got diagnosed that it dawned on me. We discussed it further and we both could totally see why people felt negatively and turned away from Christ when times get dark. *The wickedness of this world sucks! Why would He allow such a thing to happen to us? What did we do to possibly deserve this?* Sure, we questioned the Lord on why this was happening to our family, but we never questioned His goodness.

In fact, we should have been welcoming of such wrath. Cancer or worse should have been our punishment over and over again, but Christ took that beating. Jesus's blood paid the price for it all, and He took our place instead. We should have been doomed to misery. And yet He honors us with grace and favor. He washed our filthy sins white as snow, and thankfully we get to spend eternity in paradise with Him. That reward alone is worth the risk to trust and follow Him forever.

This journey or even my life up until this point could've been so much simpler if I were to point a finger and damn the Lord, but I've learned that it's actually so much easier to surrender by giving it all to Him. Letting Him fight my battles and be my Defender takes the pressure off of me entirely. I'm not saying that I apply this entire chapter perfectly in everything that I do. But the thought that I don't have to know it all, because He does, is far less stressful. Trusting that He is in charge and has control over my next season doesn't seem quite as overwhelming. I don't have to be perfect, because He is! When your eyes are fixed on Christ, it feels like you're walking on water.

chapter twelve

August 17, 2020

This is an excerpt from my journal that I wrote on August 17, 2020, at 11:13 p.m.

Something very strange just happened to me as I was taking a shower and reflecting on this long day. Today we attempted to get out of the house by going out to our favorite local pizza joint, Donatos, with some friends, but I ended up taking Cody home early due to him not feeling too well. My hopes were crushed that he wasn't feeling well enough to enjoy our much-needed outing.

When I sat down on the shower bench, all I could do was replay today's conversations. Some were good and some were not so good. I was paralyzed in deep thought, but I still sought to seek God's face, voice, and will. I needed His help.

It's unexplainable, really. I was pulled out of a deep, deep trance by a voice that firmly cried out, "Jackie!" Assuming Cody had woken up, I quickly came to, stood up, and waited for my name to be called upon again. Nothing . . .

"Did you call my name?" I yelled back to my husband, who had previously been asleep when I had gotten in. I opened up the shower door and stuck my head out, waiting for his response. Nothing . . .

Okay . . . So then I began to get nervous out of fear that he had fallen or needed my immediate help. I left the shower running, hopped out, and walked swiftly into the bedroom, not even giving myself time to grab a towel to catch the dripping water. I stood there cold and soaked only to find my husband still peacefully snoring in bed. Odd! I resumed my shower, but the more I thought about it, it became unsettling. I was 100 percent sure that I heard my name being called. I started to panic, thinking someone else was in our house. As soon as I shut the water off, I wrapped myself in a towel, grabbed my handgun, and did a sweep of the house, but found no one. It was too freaky! My name was called upon vividly—I was sure of it.

Just as I pulled back the covers to settle into bed, I felt a nudge tell me that my night wasn't over. I felt the urge to write about this experience. Now I'm sitting here thinking . . . Lord, did You call my name? If so, I hear You. What do You want from me?

A friend randomly called me today, giving me a word that popped into his spirit tonight that he thought I should know.

"Jackie, the Lord wants you to know that you are known. And He sees you," he proclaimed. "Nothing you are doing is going unnoticed. You are doing great."

I was flattered and appreciated this message, but I didn't necessarily care about being seen.

God, I really don't care about being noticed, but I'm thankful to be pleasing You. Can you just heal Cody?

P.S. As I sit here at my dining room table, ready to close this book for the night and head to sleep, I am now staring at a new sign decor I bought today from Walmart. It reads: "Pray without ceasing. 1 Thessalonians 5:17."

Is this why You've called me to this moment? Should I be praying and talking to You even more? Should I be pressing even deeper into You? Food for thought . . . Now you got me thinking, God . . . Have Your way with me until I breathe my last breath.

—Daughter of the King

chapter thirteen

Best Foot Forward

His uncle's wedding on August 22, 2020, will always be unforgettable. Number one, because Cody's Uncle Daniel, whose nickname is Sugaman, married the love of his life, the beautiful Detia, who has also become one of my closest friends. And number two, because Cody was an absolute trooper.

My husband was weak. He had been losing a lot of weight, and he had taken some drastic steps back from his everyday routine. His colleague had completely taken over his practice, and his gym days were becoming fewer and farther between. The fire and determination were still in his eyes, but there was no hiding the exhaustion. Honestly, I begged him for us to stay home if he wasn't feeling well enough to participate in this wedding, but he wasn't taking no for an answer. His feet seemed to be swelling more and more each day. And I didn't think it was smart for him to be standing all day participating in all of the groomsman festivities. I feared that he wouldn't be able to make the roughly eight-hour trip down to Moultrie, Georgia. How could this be more important than his health? Or his life, for that matter? However, he assured me that as long as he was still breathing, we were going.

Remember how I told you he was dangerously loyal? This was a moment of just that. When Cody loved you, he *loved* you. In his heart, that loyalty was locked in for life. He and his uncle were very close—Sugaman was someone my husband looked up to very much. There was no way in the world he would've wanted this day to be anything shy from perfect for this man.

On the Thursday leading up to the weekend, we began our journey south towards our halfway marker, Marietta, Georgia. My parents had moved there right around Cody's diagnosis date. We decided that breaking up the drive and spending the night with them would be in our best interest. We hadn't seen their new house yet, so this was also the perfect opportunity to visit with them. They were overjoyed and looking forward to hosting us.

Once we arrived, Cody noticed that his feet had almost doubled in size from not having his feet propped up in the car. He was so nonchalant and tranquil about it, but I was freaking out. Nurturing my husband and ensuring his comfort was all that mattered to me at the time, but my whole heart crumbled, feeling conflicted about us making the trip.

We ran the bathtub and filled it with Epsom salt for him to soak, in hopes that it would soothe his feet. He didn't complain, despite the tiresome demeanor he wore. When finished, he simply smiled, laughed, and continued to visit with my folks. Around bedtime, we elevated his feet and surrounded him with pillows for comfort.

The next morning his legs looked much better. The swelling had gone down tremendously. We laid in bed for a bit to discuss how the weekend would look, and I inquired about how he was feeling. He convinced me that he was fine, so we moved on to being optimistic and excited. Within minutes of him sitting upright and vertically hitting the floor, his feet swelled up again like two balloons. My man just couldn't catch a break! I instantly became discouraged and wept for him. But he promised me that they didn't hurt and urged me to pay them no mind. Cody would always remain calm and was easygoing about each symptom his body experienced. This made it hard for me to differentiate the seriousness in his condition unless I called his doctor, which I did quite frequently.

Once we hopped in the car to drive further down the Peach State, Cody rested while I made several calls to his doctors to update them on his condition and recent symptoms. I was worried by their concerns. Nonetheless, I listened to the rest of Priscilla Shirer's audiobook, *Fervent*. She was on fire and speaking directly to my soul. God was working on something *big*. And I could feel it.

Upon our arrival, you would never have thought that my husband had cancer. He was acting like a brand-new man! His laugh was contagious, and his conversations seemed normal. His appetite was huge, and a smile never left his face. He made sure that the attention was completely off of his situation and solely on the happy couple. I caught myself keeping my eyes locked on him, waiting for him to give me the "I'm okay" look.

Everything about that weekend was wonderful from rehearsal to reception. There were light rain showers the morning of the big day. But I comforted the bride by telling her this rain meant good luck for their marriage. There was faint drizzling the morning of our wedding, too, and we were told that it was good luck because once a knot becomes wet, it's extremely hard to untie. Thankfully that afternoon, the weather was gorgeous and sunny just in time for a bride's dream day.

Detia looked breathtaking coming down the aisle! There was love in the air, and everyone looked lovely. We were surrounded by amazing company, and the day as a whole was nothing shy of perfection. What a beautiful start to a beautiful marriage! We felt overwhelmingly thankful to be a part of such a monumental day.

Truthfully, I had forgotten. I forgot in those moments that my husband was ill. I was reassured by the way he stood next to his uncle—straight, confident, handsome, tall, and proud. And

when he led the groomsmen into the reception after their introduction, he boldly danced! Let me tell you—he broke it DOWN
on that dance floor. He was putting his best foot forward and
wearing the armor of God for strength. It didn't dawn on me
that he was using all of his might to seem okay and pull through
the night. He wore the pain well, because it fooled even me.

It wasn't until halfway through the reception that my mind
stepped back into our reality. I noticed Cody sitting more while
the other guys were standing. His enthusiasm was slowly starting to deplete while the others were just beginning to turn it
up. I wanted to hold him and encourage him to come with me
and for us to go lay it down for the night, but I didn't think he
would allow me to kill the mood. It wasn't until he gave me a
look other than the "I'm okay" look that I knew he truly wasn't
well. The look he gave me screamed that he was in trouble.

Once he gave me the green light that he was ready to go, we
left the reception early and headed back to the hotel, where he
could get some much-needed rest. If he'd let me have my way,
we would have gone straight to the emergency room prior to
going to the hotel. But my husband was hella stubborn. He didn't
realize until later that I had been in contact all weekend with
his doctors and updating his medical team on his symptoms as
they would trigger. They were very gracious in being on standby
not only during the week, but on weekends, too, as I called them
multiple times a day with questions and concerns.

The following day after the wedding, we made the seven-hour trip to Nashville, Tennessee, where we would be admitted into the Vanderbilt University Medical Center, again. We stopped halfway at my parent's house to reposition Cody with lots of pillows and blankets. Making the stop allowed him to stretch his legs, and we laid down the back seat for him where we created a comfy pallet bed for him to snooze on. He looked comfortable, and I was grateful he was able to nap during the ride.

On August 26, after a couple of days admitted into the hospital, the doctors decided it was best if we discontinued all treatment for his cancer indefinitely, pharmaceutically and holistically, in hopes that his body would naturally recover. We were extremely discouraged. This decision left us feeling like sitting ducks in a pond with hidden, lurking hunters all around ready to take us out at any moment.

Fast-forwarding a bit towards the end of his fight, I later explained to his doctors and medical team all about how he was just dancing at his uncle's wedding in late August. They were in pure amazement and had a hard time believing me. They explained to me that a tumor of that magnitude, and a cancer as aggressive as his, should have been nearly impossible for him to remain mobile, let alone dance the night away.

Cody's heart was immaculate. When he had his mind made up to do something, he did it, and he usually did it well. The strength he possessed was unimaginable. It had to have come straight from above, because it did not make sense to the human mind. "Giving up" did not belong in his vocabulary. His determination was admirable, and his mentality was solid. Starting way before cancer invaded his body, this was Cody Keon Eubanks!

chapter fourteen

September 22, 2020

This is an excerpt from my journal that I wrote on September 22, 2020, at 8:43 p.m. while Cody was admitted into the Vanderbilt University Medical Center.

The Lord just showed me something extraordinary. Mark the date 9/22. This is the first day of fall. On this day we are to harvest our blessings from the previous season. We are to harvest the fruit of our laboring. Catch this . . . As I'm praying over my husband's body as he sleeps, my heart is shattered, and my flesh is numb. For the first time ever words like fire are rolling off of my tongue as I speak aloud to Father God. I find a secret place with Him. I see all purple, and I know He is covering the room thick with His presence. I'm broken, I'm weak, I'm hurt, I'm scared, all I want is for my Cody to be healed. I would take his place in a heartbeat without a second of hesitation if I could. Lord, why him? My soul aches for him to be well again. God showed me this as I'm in tears and wailing over my husband's body.

God showed me that He was me, and Cody was the church—Cody was the Lord's people. Cody was me . . . God would do anything to take our place—in fact, He did take our place. He died in our place. He took our punishment so we wouldn't have to. He was the true martyr, so I don't have to be on behalf of my husband. He has felt all of this sorrow and agony before. He has experienced every single detail from every point of view. He goes before us, He walks beside us, and He is always behind us. There's no shadow where He won't find us.

BAM! There He goes, blowing my mind once again. Stop worrying. Stop fearing, Jackie. Cody is well because Christ is well. The same resurrection power that raised Jesus Christ, the son of God, from the grave, runs in the veins of my precious Cody. He will not die but live to tell of this miracle and spread glory about the kingdom and the Healer that heals.

When I looked up after my special vision, I saw multiple crosses. My favorite was how Cody's body was in the shape of a cross. My soul felt pure joy. God's heart aches for his children way more than my heart aches for my husband. Jesus was tempted and tried. And so are we. He beat it and so can we.

chapter fifteen

Submerged Healing

After he had been discharged from the hospital for the third time now, Cody's new pain medicine made him sleep and sleep and sleep and sleep some more.

I must admit, despite how unsettling those hospital stays had become, I never complained to or in front of my husband, nor left his side for an extended period of time. Out of all three hospital stays, Aunt Flo came into town each time. How had I gotten so lucky by her appearance three times in a row? I don't know, but I didn't find it amusing. The abdominal cramps were not fun, but I remained quiet and still when by his side. The guest chairs that pulled out into beds were excruciatingly uncomfortable to sleep on. My body and especially my neck would ache for days after our stays. The way I looked at it was, if Cody wasn't complaining, neither would I. His condition trumped mine and how I felt by 500 percent. With Cody's body raging in heat to fight off the illness inside of him, we often kept the room freezing cold. This meant that no matter how many layers or blankets I put on, my fingers and toes were still numb. I often went to warm up outside, but sometimes the weather didn't cooperate.

Even though my husband didn't mind, I wasn't such a fan of sitting days on end in my own stench. On this third go-around, I made a special trip home from Nashville to Bowling Green for a real estate closing as an excuse to shower in my own privacy. After that quick shower and work run, I turned right back around to nestle into my love's arms. I hated to have left his side. And how could I dare complain about these minuscule things while he was dealing with something far greater than I was?

At one point, Cody had been telling the doctors for a couple days that his pain level was an 8/10 on the pain tolerance scale. Our care team had spent these days experimenting and adjusting his new pain medicine. Several of these medicines made him nauseous, so there were periods when he could only hold down ice chips. Anytime Cody was awake, I would hop in his hospital bed and curl up beside him or sit on the foot of his bed with my feet in his lap, facing him. The medicine would soon kick in and knock him out again, so we utilized this time by giving one another our undivided attention.

I remember him once sitting there with such a big grin on his face while eating those bland ice chips. They surely couldn't have been that satisfying, but my man devoured them like they were steaks. He was being so goofy as he inhaled each single chip. He would hold his pinky finger high in the air, give me a lustful look, and then pop in each piece to make me laugh. And we laughed uncontrollably at his silliness. Something this simple brought us unexplainable joy despite the horrid circumstances. No matter the pain, he expressed to the nurses that he felt we still made the most of every moment we were given together. He truly made the best of the hardest trials.

Another time, Cody slept for eighteen hours straight without waking up. Legitimately, I would nudge him a couple of times just to receive a mild groan for confirmation that he hadn't conked out indefinitely. Sometimes, I would wake him and stick a straw in his mouth just to make sure he took in some water, so he wouldn't get too dehydrated. Cody sleeping this much would scare the daylights out of me, but I convinced myself that his body needed this rest to heal and recover. He took 20mg of Oxycodone on top of 20mg of OxyContin to ease his pain, plus all the other ten-plus pills he was steadily taking for stability was doping him up so badly that he didn't have much energy to do anything but rest.

Within these few days back at home, I was extremely unproductive. Every ounce of attention I had was glued on counting his snores. I was latched to his side. I didn't feel like I could properly eat, sleep, work, cook, read, talk . . . nothing! My everything was paralyzed and shut down. I wasn't sleeping at all, but my definition of rest had become watching him breathe in and out. I often sat at the foot of his recliner for hours in silence. There I would pray, rub his swollen legs and feet, scroll social media on my phone, or simply stare at him and analyze his demeanor. I would sit by his side for hours, watching the veins in his neck pulse. I found peace in counting the beats per minute. This was so soothing to me. He was still here with me, and I was thankful for those moments.

Friends and family did their best to deter my focus, but my focal point was on my husband. Everyone wanted to visit him, but I had to be sneaky in arranging company to come by when he was asleep, because when he would wake up, he didn't want any visitors. Cody didn't want anyone to see him in this weak, vulnerable state, but I needed other bodies around to keep myself from going crazy.

After a long day of his resting, I loved when he would finally wake up, because those were the moments I waited for all day. I would get so excited with jolts of energy, doing anything and everything he needed or wanted me to do at the sound of his request. Bringing him food, getting him a drink, handing him medicine, and showering him with plenty of hugs and kisses. He was my person, and I wanted to please him.

On September 26 in particular, the Spirit led me to be creative with our healing requests. I invited my husband to join me in our two-person bathtub, but he was feeling too weak to put in the effort of getting in and out of the tub. For a moment, I was disappointed by the rejection, because I had loved how *this* had become our thing. Epsom salt bubble baths had become one of our favorite ways to spend time with one another since moving into our new house. It was enjoyable to sit there in his presence, plus his body needed the detox and relaxation.

Since he would not be joining me this time, I lit two candles to signify my purpose of soaking alone. I sparked one for Cody that said *healing* on the side and lit one for me that said *strength and energy*. I stared at the flames for what seemed like forever. Their small torches burned beautifully, and I imagined their fuse never going out. I began to pray, and I prayed for these attributes to submerge us.

Lord, give Cody complete healing. Please, please, please. Restore the cells in his body and make them brand new. Kill anything that isn't holy. And engulf anything that doesn't belong to You. Please continue to give me Your supernatural strength and Your unending energy for this season, God. Help me to continue honoring You in everything that I do. Hold my hand as I navigate deep waters and walk through the trenches of uncertainty. Prince of Peace, please don't leave us. We need You.

From the bath, I listened to soft worship music and watched as my husband slept peacefully in his chair. I sat in there for over an hour, reflecting on this journey and praying for guidance to proceed. I begged for God to have His way and nothing less.

Before getting out, I decided to slip back on my original wedding rings. At the time, I wore a pink rubber band in their place because my actual rings would hurt Cody when I massaged his legs. Our wedding rings symbolize us being one flesh and the holy union we share. I used these to stand in Cody's place on his behalf for the sacrifice that was to come. Still praying unceasingly for healing over his temple, I held my nose and submerged my entire flesh into the warm water. When I arose, I declared that full healing had taken place within my husband's being—in Jesus's name. Amen.

Just as the night was falling and I was preparing to settle in for the night myself, my husband woke up full of energy. This hadn't been the case for the past couple of days, so I was thrilled. Had my prayers worked? *Thank you, God!* Cody told me that he wanted Taco Bell, or Taco Smell as we liked to call it, for dinner. *Woah!* He hadn't been eating well either, so for him to not only request, but order and finish everything on the menu was a big deal to us. I was over the moon thankful for his enthusiasm, effort, and stability. He looked really good!

Before leaving the house to grab food, I instinctively texted our mentors at the time to let them know Cody's status and that he wanted Taco Smell for dinner! They were beyond shocked as well and asked if he might come over for a change of scenery. I was reluctant to ask Cody myself, so I had one of them pitch the idea on speakerphone. He was enthused and agreed to this unexpected, last hangout with their whole family at their house.

My husband seemed genuinely happy to be sitting on the couch in the midst of his favorite people. We didn't stay too long, but while we were there, we shared laughs and spoke openly. To me, he looked great, but towards the end of our stay, Cody requested his pain medicine. I held out giving it to him for as long as I could, because I loved seeing him awake, alert, and full of life while not on the medication. I knew the rest of the night would go downhill once he took it. *Be still, my heart*, I thought as I reluctantly handed him the pills.

As a result, his speech began to slur, and he needed his mentor's assistance getting to the car and back in our house. Cody is still hands down the strongest person I've come to know, despite the rough night we endured afterwards.

chapter sixteen

Satan Comes to Steal, Kill, and Destroy

Early on in our courting, several people questioned my relationship with Cody. The lack of respect others had in my decision-making truly bothered me, especially when I knew what we had was rare. Years later, just weeks before I was about to marry the love of my life, I dealt with another series of people who questioned our relationship and my faith.

In 2018–2019, I periodically attended a small, intimate meditation group containing maybe five to seven women. I was introduced to this outing by a local business owner after a long conversation we had about my love for the Lord. I briefly expressed to him how I lived such a fast-paced life but wanted to slow it down so I could be more intentional about spending time with Christ throughout my busy week. He then pointed me in the direction of this group that met each Wednesday around lunchtime for one hour. I was under the assumption that it would be Christian-based meditation based on his suggestions to my desires. He was very adamant about how this intentionally uninterrupted hour could help me learn how to still my mind and hone in on what was really important in life. This sounded like just what I needed at the time. And it was—for a while.

While sitting cross-legged on a doughy pillow in a circle with other women around, I solely dedicated this quiet, relaxing, uninterrupted time to focus on my King and grow deeper in Him. With our eyes softly closed, this time became sacred and holy to me. It allowed me to quietly and privately seek, pray, confess, and open up before my Heavenly Father. This gave me the stillness to press completely into Him. The peace I felt by sitting still before Him in the midst of the throne room was priceless, and the atmosphere was so freeing.

Also, I loved not feeling alone. I was surrounded by other women while dedicating this tranquil time to Him. The majority of these ladies were much older than me, and they seemed at the time to be much wiser, too. They often spoke of a higher spiritual backing, which I had assumed was the same as my ideology. I was always extremely bold in expressing my faith and love for Jesus Christ, and they were always very supportive. Because of this, I never paid attention to the faint red flags.

Cody found this group to be a bit odd from the beginning, but he encouraged me to keep going since it made me feel closer and more connected to Christ. Although it wasn't in his nature to express his love, faith, and walk with Jesus charismatically, he respected and understood when others would. He could point out someone with ill intentions from a mile away, and truly had the gift of discernment. But me being on the naïve side, I had assumed everyone in this weekly gathering believed in Christ, too. I thought we were all on the same page in proclaiming truth in the Holy Bible—the same doctrine that I study and believe. Since they encouraged me to openly speak about my Prince and never deterred down another path, I could only presume that they were using their time for this purpose as well. It wasn't until only weeks before my and Cody's wedding date that I learned the hard way that they did not share my faith.

One afternoon I was invited to hang out one-on-one with a lady from the group. Casually enjoying a conversation about who-knows-what, our topic of discussion shifted.

"I've never gotten the opportunity to share something with you, Jackie. Do you care if I enlighten you on my spiritual beliefs?" she asked, while taking another sip of her drink.

I have always been a sucker for meaningful, stimulating conversations. Surface-level talk never seems to challenge me, so the deeper the conversations the better in my eyes.

"Sure!" I replied.

Once she began to share, something in the atmosphere felt *off*. I felt cold chills going down my spine, and my palms began to grow clammy. I tried to be open-minded and respect her difference in opinions and beliefs, and she proceeded telling me how a couple other girls in our meditation group shared her same or similar beliefs. But what shook me was once she pointed to a speck on her countertop.

"This is the God you serve compared to what I believe. He is small in the grand scheme of things," she said.

Instantly, in my heart I became defensive of His great name. I quietly waited for my turn to speak, but inside I was raging and ready to lovingly combat her with what the Word says to be true. In my heart, I *knew* God wasn't just a speck on a countertop. He was the whole damn thing!

After wholeheartedly listening and waiting patiently, I spoke.

"Thank you for sharing your beliefs with me. I respect you, but I don't recall that that's what the Bible says to be true." Then I began to question. "If Christians have the Bible as reference, where are you getting this knowledge from? Where are your beliefs sourced from? What keeps you grounded in this belief?"

Then as I was just barely getting started in defending His name and questioning why she believed what she did, she nonchalantly led me to the front door and showed me out. It was the oddest thing . . . no dispute or any confrontation—just possible tension, because I felt unheard after listening to her hour-long spill. I didn't even get my chance to justify the Truth!

Anyways, I was so disturbed that I took the scenic route home. Although she was rather convincing, surely she couldn't be right. I needed time to clear my head before facing my fiancé at the time. I needed to think. I needed to breathe. I needed to pray, but instead of peacefully praying, I found myself yelling to God for clarity. I was so shaken up! If anything that she was telling me from our conversation was true, I begged that He reveal it to me immediately. I remember crying hysterically, confused. I didn't know what else to do to calm down, so I started to sing.

The first song that popped into my spirit was "So Will I" by Hillsong Worship, so I began to praise Him aloud in my car. And the lyrics to this song were so fitting. My spirit rested on these last three words of the chorus: "So will I." For some God-known reason, I couldn't stop meditating on those three delicate words. I repeated them around in my mouth a few times.

"So will I. So will I. So will I."

I caught myself speeding up the tongue and repeatedly saying that phrase faster and faster. All my energy was forced into replicating *So will I*, until it clicked.

So will I. So will I. So a lie. So a LIE!

Bam! Once this dawned on me, my tears of confusion turned into tears of rejoicing and thanksgiving. In that moment, our sovereign Maker showed me that that conversation was not the truth. It was "so a lie!" I am incredibly grateful that when He pursued me, my heart listened and received His truth. Also, the Lord didn't need me to defend Him because He can defend Himself.

The following week during meditation, my soul just wasn't in it. All I could think about was that conversation and how it was so a lie. How could I sit there and pretend this group was for me, if the meditation leader herself was not on the same page with Christ? I enjoyed this time, but was I entangled with the wrong crowd? Was I supposed to continue going? But because I am as stubborn as they come, I went back the third following week. I still treasured this time I was dedicating to Christ, so I thought maybe I could get over our differences and continue to press forward. After all, everyone is entitled to their own opinion.

Thankfully, I felt super connected to Christ that day. I saw His Kingdom purple dancing around and loving all over me while in meditation. I was only two weeks away from the special day when I would be wed and become Mrs. Eubanks. All was well with the world, and her opinions were the least of my worries.

Unexpectedly, Satan showed up! And the Lord answered my questions about if this was the place for me. Before leaving, that same woman and another elderly lady decided they needed to have an important intervention with me. As we were still huddled in a circle, sitting crisscross on pillows, out of the blue they began expressing to me how they thought I shouldn't marry Cody. Without voicing much reason at all, they felt as if he wasn't the man for me.

What!? Let me remind you that this was TWO weeks before our big day. None of them in the group had ever met my Cody, and I couldn't recall a time that I'd belittled him to make them think otherwise. I must be honest—this brief conversation with them spooked the daylights out of me. They were good women, just lost and clueless about our relationship. But because of them being much older than me, I became frightened that they might have known or seen something that I did not. They had been outspoken without any knowledge of any facts.

Plus, this was a very crucial time in my life. Marrying someone is a lifelong commitment and shouldn't be taken lightly. And them planting those seeds of doubt alarmed me. Through the words and actions of these women, Satan was trying to manipulate and destroy a precious union before it even got started.

Needless to say, I confided this to Cody, and we discussed my cold feet moment in premarital counseling together. It was a huge blessing for me to get the heck out of that meditation group; but on the flip side, I will be forever thankful for that season in my life, because it drew me deeper and closer to our Lord yet again. If I had fallen for Satan's sneaky, devious plan, God would not have been able to work his magic through mine and Cody's marriage. I may not have been there for Cody's toughest hour or him there for many of mine. If we had listened to the toxic murmurs around us, perhaps our faith would not be standing this strong.

The devil hates a Christ-centered marriage, and we were a power couple unified by Him! Satan was steadily trying to destroy another one of God's great plans and what He had in store. Certainly evil viewed us as a threat. We were truly better together, and God had put together a great team. If God is for us, who can stand against us? No one and nothing, that's who! Not even death.

chapter seventeen

Timeline

Part One: **Monday, September 28**

We had been waiting on this day for months. It was treatment day! Cody had been off of treatment for a couple of months now, due to a negative reaction to the immunotherapy. Doctors wanted to hold off on treatment until now to calm down the inflammation in his liver. His liver had become super swollen, not only from the cancer, but from it being attacked with medicine. Needless to say, we were so excited to get back in the swing of things and for Cody to be on the road to recovery. But Cody was noticeably weak this morning.

Only two days prior, I had woken up in the middle of the night to the sound of my love throwing up. When I bounced out of bed to investigate, he was hunched over the toilet seat in agony. Noticing the shower turned on, lights turned off, and the bathroom ventilation fans going, I wondered why he hadn't woken me. I wondered what had sparked this vomiting episode, which would resume for the days to come. Once he had finished and we cleaned him up, I grabbed us blankets and pillows and took a seat beside him on the bathroom floor.

"Babe, why is the shower running, fans going, and lights not on?" I asked out of curiosity, wanting to play catch-up on what I had missed.

"I didn't want to wake you," he replied.

I couldn't help but grin just a little. I definitely needed the sleep, and his acknowledgment of this was thoughtful. But didn't he realize my dedication in never wanting to leave his side?

"We are a team. I am in this with you," I assured him.

Even during a time when it should've been all about him, he was still taking care of me.

At dawn, a friend brought a wheelchair over to our house for us to use throughout the course of the day. During our last trip to Vanderbilt for lab work, Cody couldn't walk very far or fast without needing a minute to catch his breath. I couldn't bear seeing him this way, so during one of our rest stops on a nearby bench, I fibbed a little and said I'd be right back after the restroom or something. When I was out of his sight, I ran up and down the hospital hallways seeking a wheelchair for my beloved. He would never have asked for it or accepted it, but he couldn't refuse, and was grateful when I rounded the corner with it in my possession.

Since Cody had just had another rough night, I needed assistance in getting him to the car. My back was a bit sore at this point from lifting him up on my own a few times too many. So I called two of our other friends around 8:00 a.m., and they came over on extremely short notice to help get him in the car. They showered him with love and respect. We were still blessed.

That particular hour-long car ride down to Nashville was more nerve-racking and gut-wrenching than the others had been. It was quite difficult to focus on the road while also holding my husband's puke bag. He was weak, but still smiling through the pain. My insides were shattered that he was not having a good morning, for this was supposed to be a great day. When he would doze off to sleep, I tried driving as cautiously as I could, but each bump or turn would break his rest. *Ugh!* I would have done anything, and I mean absolutely anything, to trade places with him. I wanted to pull over on the side of the interstate to cry, but I had to keep it together and press forward for him.

I stayed up pretty late the night before writing out a secret, detailed note to our oncologist doctor, stating and describing my concerns for him. I wanted to address to her that:

1. The new medicines were making things worse, rapidly.

2. My husband was showing signs of depression, but he would never admit it.

Cody didn't like when I asked too many questions or gave raw, detailed feedback to the doctors. He wanted me to sit there quietly while he did all of the talking, but I remained his honest advocate despite what he thought. At this point, a note was the only way to express to her what was truly going on. Once we had arrived, I slipped it to the nurse aid, telling him that it needed to reach our doctor.

Apparently, our oncologist spotted Cody in the waiting room and *knew*. What was everyone seeing that I could not? I knew Cody was in pain and not feeling well but couldn't fathom the idea of death already being at our doorstep. She had another fellow doctor tell us that our appointment was being canceled and that she would not be seeing us today. She proposed that we needed to be admitted back into the hospital immediately. She also gave word that she would come find me later to discuss my note.

We were then escorted upstairs to the infusion room, where Cody was given a bed to rest his head. Cody didn't seem to care about being admitted again, but I demanded questions as to why. All he kept asking for was more pain medicine. And when asked, he told everyone his pain level was a 10/10; but aside from the occasional throw up, his stoic demeanor didn't show much else to indicate that he was in torment. I believe no one took his severe pain seriously enough because he remained so calm. If he was supposed to be admitted again, why wasn't anyone doing anything? I was so upset with the staff, feeling that no one was giving him enough attention. I marched up and down the hallway, asking several nurses for help and to come check on him. Eventually, he was given high doses of the Oxys.

Our oncologist found us shortly after we got situated in the infusion room. She entered the room slowly, and graciously gave her warm love to Cody. She encouraged him with kind words and then hinted for me to step outside so that we could talk in private.

I am certain the conversation I had with her in those quiet, lonely halls will forever be the worst conversation I will ever have to endure.

When I confidently asked her what we were going to do to make him better now, she carefully told me, "There's *nothing* else we can do for him."

I must have looked puzzled, because she slowly began telling me that Cody was in the final stages of dying and that it was only a matter of time. She told me that I must have seen this coming, but truthfully, I had not. I knew he was in mortifying pain at times, but I didn't allow the thought of him passing to cross my mind. *Positive vibes only, right?* Cody didn't permit me to see him so low, he never complained, and he didn't show me how much the cancer was hurting or affecting him. He laughed it out or smiled with reassuring words that he would beat this and that he would be okay. I had no clue it was *this* bad.

When telling me this, my knees gave in as if chopped off at the bone. Her body and the wall to her back broke my fall. I could not bear my devastation. Her words were literally choking me, and my thoughts that followed them were unruly. All I could hear was a piercing ringing in my ears, and everything was being consumed from all around me. The walls were caving in, and I began to lose my vision. In that moment, everything was moving in slow motion, and I could not function.

In the midst of the chaos in my mind, heart, and soul, I heard the voice of God.

"Find Cody," He said.

Where is my husband? Where is my Cody? I longed to be right by his side.

Before entering his room, I had to soak up all my tears. Even though he was now in and out of sleep, it would devastate him to see me crying. *My precious Cody. My sweet, sweet man. My God-sent angel on this bloody, cursed earth.*

Gently taking his hands, I repeatedly whispered, "Death will not take you, my love. You will be healed."

There was no way I could be the one to tell my husband this horrid news. I didn't believe, couldn't stomach, or even process it myself. My nerves at this point were shot, and I was running to the restroom to relieve myself at least every twenty minutes. I was panicking and couldn't just sit there in my own desperate thoughts.

I made a call to my mentor. She insisted on coming down to Nashville right away, even if it was just to sit outside on the bench, calling to update our family and friends, informing them of our latest news. After calling my mom, she came immediately to our aid, too, with my youngest sister. I called Cody's mom, and lastly his uncle. There was no way I could've given my attention to anyone else any longer for updates. Our time left together was more sacred than ever before.

After the medical team let Cody catch up on rest for a few more hours, they transferred him to another room where a young, nervous doctor broke the news to Cody. Although he wasn't entirely truthful with us about the timeframe our oncologist had given me, he handled the conversation with great empathy and compassion.

Our oncologist had said, "It was only a matter of time," implying days, while this fellow tried to pose to Cody that he had months left. Either way, I was torn. While holding my husband's hand, I held back tears and studied his body language to this dagger. He remained completely composed, just like when we were given the news about his diagnosis. In fact, the young doctor seemed more frightened than Cody.

At last, after moments of silence, Cody said in an assuring tone, "Well, that sucks, but that's more than enough time for me to beat this."

He was not accepting the given news and promised us that he still felt good, considering. My heart eased up in feeling his good spirits, knowing he still had much fight left in him.

On a much lighter note, something sweet, special, and monumental happened that evening, too. Cody and I had always been ChapStickaholics. A "ChapStickaholic" is someone who is completely obsessed with applying ChapStick. These people are a species of humans who, when ChapStick is used up, lost, or stolen, experience withdrawal symptoms, such as extreme dry or cracked lips, constant licking of the lips, patting of the lips with water, irritability, anger, and sometimes even death. As addicts, we liked to refer to ourselves as ChapStick connoisseurs and had constant fun revolved around ChapStick.

In the hospital, while applying Carmex ChapStick, I remembered a funny story that had taken place during a trip to Sebring, Florida, to visit his family. Cody, his mom, and I were in the car, driving around town to who knows where. She, being a ChapStickaholic too, said, "Can you pass me the Climax?"— instead of Carmex. After a long awkward pause, we all burst into deep laughter that made our tummies hurt at the rated-R thoughts in our minds. It was truly a had-to-be-there moment, but from that day on, we favored Carmex for the humor attached to it.

As Cody and I were sitting in our new hospital room, which would be our room for several days to come, a God-sent message popped into my head. To make my husband smile and bring joy to the moment we were given, we anointed my Carmex tube of ChapStick with holy healing powers. Every time we applied it to his lips, he would be given supernatural strength and peace within the moment. *This* particular fifteen-ounce tube was *special* to us.

Part Two: Tuesday, September 29

The doctors told us that Cody had taken a drastic turn overnight, much faster than expected. They said he didn't have much longer left, days maybe, but definitely not a week. Initially our care team looked into relocating us to a hospice center closer to home in Bowling Green but warned me of the risk that he might not be stable enough to travel. Also, there weren't any beds available at the time, so staying in Vanderbilt remained our best option. We were currently on the palliative care floor of the hospital, but they wanted to transport him upstairs to the hospice unit. Ironically, there were no more beds available on that floor either.

Several family members and friends came to see him at Vanderbilt, including his mom. I am thankful she was in the room with me when the doctor served me the do-not-resuscitate orders. As I signed them, my hand was numb and my mind foggy with the thought of actually losing him. Everyone promised that this would be for the best. His mom's presence and blessing to proceed with my signature was needed.

Peace filled the room whenever our lead pastor at our local church made the drive down to spend a crucial twenty minutes with us. Mind you that pre-COVID-19, our church contained at least 2,500 attendees per week. To say we felt important for him to come see us was an understatement.

I can't remember what our pastor rambled on and on about at first, but what really caught our attention was when I asked him, "What should Cody expect heaven to be like?"

Our pastor's face lit up like a Christmas tree. And instantly, the sun began to shine through the big hospital windows behind me and Cody. It was clear as day that the Lord guided and confirmed our pastor's response. And it was glorious.

We asked Cody how the thought of heaven made him feel. Doped up on pain medicine, his response was, "That sounds pretty fun." My heart was full of peace, knowing he would soon be in a place much sweeter than this if Christ were to call him home soon.

Not too long before this, on September 8, 2019, we had been baptized together. Cody was obediently baptized first by his mentor. Then my husband, the appointed spiritual leader of our family, baptized me, his wife, under God and all who were gathered there. It was certainly beautiful, and the Lord was pleased.

I was warned by our nurses not to expect Cody to wake up with me the next morning. He was weak and going in and out of consciousness. At one point when he was awake and alert, we had an emotional conversation together. As much as it pained me and I truly did not want to let him go, I gave him my blessing to let go if his name was being called upon in heaven. I assured him that I would find a way to be okay if the Lord was calling him home. Cody promised me that he wouldn't be going anywhere, but I told him he must dare not refuse to be face to face with Jesus Christ for the sake of me.

The darkness of this night will haunt me forever. My husband was constipated and hadn't performed a bowel movement for five days now. The suppository helped a little but didn't do the magic trick. His body needed to flush itself, but the pain medicine was clogging him up drastically. My heart melted when he took my hand while he was sitting on the bedside commode. The conversation we shared there will stick with me for as long as I shall live. He was miserable, but still my Cody. My love. My heart. My very best friend. Shortly after he threw up more than just stomach acid, the rest of his food, whatever, he threw up blood and a lot of it. So much that I was wearing it on my shirt. This broke me.

When Cody had fallen back asleep after the nightmare we had both endured, I stepped out into the hallway to breathe. I was panicking, and all the nurses swarmed me, showing sympathy and care.

"Is there anything we can do for you, sweetheart?" they would ask.

"I want my mom," I cried.

But because of COVID-19, this wing of the hospital permitted only one guest per patient to stay overnight, and I didn't feel like my request was valid. I wept, and I wept, and I wept. If you could ever see pain in someone's eyes, the nurses could surely see it in mine, because they were gracious enough to allow my mother to come up and stay with us.

Part Three: Wednesday, September 30

The doctors and nurses were amazed that Cody pulled through the night, but they were certain Cody didn't have much time left. They were still urging us to make the trip home to a local hospice center so that his family and friends could visit him there one last day, but there still weren't any beds available, and the doctors were doubtful that he would make the journey.

That day, I got a wild hair. I still wanted to have his children and carry on his legacy if there was no way he would be here much longer. We never froze any sperm or dove into this topic because we thought we had more time. I wanted to know more about testicular sperm aspiration, or TESA. This procedure would involve a needle to be inserted in the testicle, and the tissue/sperm would be extracted. He would not be strong enough to pull through out of the anesthesia, but I knew he would want this for not only me, but for his legacy.

When asking the doctors about this, it surprised everyone. Our doctors scurried around and went above and beyond for us to look into my request. I alone reached out to nearly a dozen specialists to get answers and help us with this task. I lined up everything to brace myself when having this conversation with the medical professionals. I received Cody's alert permission on video recording of him giving us permission that this was what he wanted, too. I knew my husband. This would leave him a happy, happy man.

That evening, Cody's mentor drove in to visit with him. The stay wasn't long, but I knew it meant the absolute world to him to have his closest friend's support. There was something about their friendship that sent Cody over the moon. The guidance, support, and wisdom his mentor gave filled a void in my husband that he had been carrying for a long time from lacking a close relationship with a spiritual male figure who could be a role model. Besides me, I promise you, his mentor was his favorite person on the planet.

Once he finished up in the room with Cody, he came to find me sitting down on a bench outside of the hospital. That conversation was a blur to me, but I do remember him suggesting that I get a notebook and start writing down any questions that I might have for my husband. He, too, warned me that the end was near.

"What should I ask him?" I asked.

After a long moment of silence, he replied, "Anything you've always wanted to know."

Within minutes of him planting the notebook seed, my older sister and my mom drove up to find us sitting in the dusk on that hospital bench. God blew my mind once again when my sister got out to hand me a beautiful notebook with the 1 John 1:5 verse on the front cover, and of course, a purple pen. Out of all the colors in the rainbow, Cody and I had been holding the color purple close to our hearts, because Jesus wore purple. How much more confirmation does one need about God's sovereignty?

That night I asked Cody all kinds of questions: "Who inspires you? What would you like your arrangements to be? What was the best day of your life? What are you going to say when you see Jesus? How can I continue to honor you? What am I supposed to do without you?"

In the meantime, I was begging the Lord to have mercy not only on my love, but on my heart that was literally crumbling from the inside out.

Part Four: Thursday, October 1

Thank you, Jesus, for another day with my husband! Through Christ and Christ alone, Cody was defeating the odds left and right. His care team was amazed by his strength, and all of them were super intrigued with our story and love for God. The staff would come by just to see if he was still breathing and hear more of our journey.

On this day in particular, I was overwhelmingly thankful that despite COVID-19, I was able to remain by my husband's side. It pained me to hear talk of other couples and family members in the hospital hallways being separated or treated harshly. I was thankful for the staff we had been blessed with and their genuine care in making sure we could be together.

Two female doctors decided to have an intervention with me regarding the TESA procedure. They took me upstairs to an old, quiet, long, dark, carpeted hallway where we sat on the floor to have the conversation. They were extremely shocked that my husband was still breathing. They were also worried that I might get too invested in the procedure and feel too much heartbreak if we couldn't pull it off. I assured them that my peace with everything had come quite some time ago when we decided to surrender all that we are to the cause of Christ. His plan would be good, and I would trust Him.

I would like to think that I perplexed them with my responses to their concerns. They didn't understand my level of faith or have responses to this new, unknown desire for our family. I shared about my relationship with the Lord and how He was still endlessly pursuing me and Cody vibrantly. They mentioned that I was more prepared for the conversation than they were, and that my young age kept tugging at everyone's hearts. One doctor held my hands and said that I reminded her of her little sister. The care they expressed and took to pause their busy day, just to show concern and spend at least thirty minutes with me, was a true gift. We took Cody still hanging on as a sign to move forward in getting more answers. I showed them the video of my husband giving consent after I let him know he was being recorded, in case he was unresponsive later. They were astonished. They disclosed that every urologist in Tennessee now knew about our story, and that everyone was looking into this request on our behalf. It was a long-shot request indeed, but it was well worth the try.

Many people drove to Vanderbilt to visit him on this day and throughout the week. My dad, Sugaman, and Detia made the trip in from Georgia, along with countless family and friends from Bowling Green flowing in and out to give their love and support.

This night in particular was a beautiful night, having two of Cody's groomsmen there to make him smile. We also had two different churches that didn't know about the other on speakerphone in our hospital room, praying unceasingly for Cody's miraculous healing. An anointed towel was brought down as well to lay over his body and suck the cancer dry. Can you believe that Cody asked for spaghetti for dinner after not eating or holding anything down all week? This tickled us all. The Spirit was moving, and all could feel His presence.

Part Five: Friday, October 2

This morning started out rough, yet full of peace. The nurse woke me up really early, around 4:00 a.m., and hinted to me that it was time. I didn't want him to continue suffering, and I was prepared again to say goodbye. God had given me several extra days with him that I will be forever grateful for. I got in bed with him and nestled into his arms. I cuddled my better half in a state of tranquility, as we awaited his passing. I quietly cried myself back to sleep, holding him probably a bit too tight.

Next thing I knew, I woke up around 7:00 a.m. to find my warrior still fighting strong. None of us knew what to think, *but God!* The medical team gushed about how they had no answers or reasoning for any of it other than his heart was stronger than his body. The hospital got a call that a hospice bed in Bowling Green had opened up, and suggested that we take it. Again, I was warned that the probability of him making the trip was slim, but they encouraged me to take it despite the odds.

Before loading up into the ambulance, our nurse told us that we had made a huge impact there in the hospital. She was doubting her profession and turning to faith because of us. She told us how people in the hallways were talking about our story. They could only imagine how amazing Cody would've been in his prime to be shining this bright in such gloomy days. If only they knew!

I was a nervous wreck for the entire ambulance ride. The only thing bringing me comfort was his hand in mine. I kept myself occupied by humming the tunes of our favorite gospel songs. Occasionally, I would question the paramedic about his experiences or Cody's vitals. Meanwhile, I never took my eyes off of Cody's heartbeat or the pulse in his neck. Every time we hit a bump or the paramedic moved, even if it was to itch his head, my heart sunk deep into my chest. The few times Cody's eyes did open, he immediately locked them with mine.

My mom drove my car behind us and aggressively followed the ambulance every inch of the way, and we had prayer warriors praying for Cody's travel home. Amazingly, his vitals were completely stable the entire ride. Praise God that we made it back home to Bowling Green!

Word travels quickly when you're as adored by the world as Cody. It seemed like everyone in town wanted to express their love to us. At least fifty people came to see him in person when we got there, and hundreds if not thousands more were praying in their own spaces. *Thank you, Jesus, for Your love and Your promises.*

chapter eighteen

Our Love

I'll never forget a rather detailed conversation I had with Cody one cozy afternoon after work. As he was sitting in his recliner and I was sitting on his lap, I gazed deep into his eyes.

"Babe, you remind me of Jesus," I actually said out loud, though it had just been a thought.

He looked at me in confusion while waiting on me to elaborate further.

I said, "It's just that I've never loved anyone more than I love you in my entire life. This is the highest form of love I know that my flesh can actually grasp. I know I'm supposed to love God more, but our love can be physical and visible always, while Christ's love is incomprehensible. Sometimes I compare the love I have for you and tie it directly to loving Him. Make sense?"

It was hard for me to tell if he felt insulted on Jesus's behalf or if he was processing his response. That conversation got rather extensive, but I remember one comment he made in particular.

"I encourage you to work on separating us two and loving Him more," he said. "I will fail you time and time again, but He will not."

It was hard for me to wrap my head around loving God more for a long time, because my love for my mate often felt infinite and superior. Cody and I were like magnets towards one another, attracting the other on every level—spiritually, romantically, emotionally, mentally, and physically. He moved, I moved. I ached, he ached. He smiled, I smiled. And when our flesh wouldn't display it always, our souls would intercede on our behalf. We were constantly thirsting for one another's presence while still obtaining individual independence. I often joked to him that he was like a drug to me that I was *highly* addicted to. There was a greater force behind us being together that was nothing short of divine intervention, which we couldn't explain to others. Our desire to have one another came solely from above.

Of course, like any couple, Cody and I definitely had our fair share of arguments throughout our relationship. We bickered about him leaving the toilet seat up or biting his fingernails. I remember getting agitated with him over what seems so silly now. As a protector, he saw snakes in the grass when I did not, which led to what I thought was him "daddying me." We argued about finances. We quarreled about money, because we would give it all away and not have enough left for our own household or our own bills at times.

I still remember our first disagreement like it was yesterday. Our dispute was over toilet paper. Oh, the irony in that now, dealing with the COVID-19 pandemic! I was over at his place, and after using the restroom, I decided to replace the toilet paper, since I had used the last of the roll. Without even thinking, because this was never a topic I put any thought towards, I inserted the roll "the wrong way." He became insanely passionate over this simple act. I learned a lot that day. I now know that the correct way to install a toilet paper roll is to have the loose end draped over the top.

One of our biggest arguments was over my own insecurities. We went downtown to a local bar to hang out with friends. He kept buying endless drinks for me and my attractive girlfriend. Well, I was three sheets to the wind already, and my jealousy kicked in over him paying for her beverages, too. You would have thought he kicked my dog with how mad I got at him. I later learned that he was only doing what he thought was the gentleman thing to do by not making the ladies open their own wallets. I also learned that too much alcohol isn't good for anybody.

On our way home that night, I demanded that he let me out of the car. About a mile away from our apartment, I flung open the car door and began belligerently stumbling home. Cody trailed me in his car the entire way. Looking back at it now, I was overreacting way more than I should have over something so insignificant, but intoxicated me wasn't seeing the situation clearly. Once we made it home, I insisted on packing my bags and leaving. As I was putting clothes into a suitcase, Cody grabbed his keys and left. When I woke up the next morning, I learned that he had gone back to the bar simply to find my friend and apologize if he had made her feel as if he were being flirtatious. He told her that he was into me and nobody else, and sorry if he had given her the wrong impression. This particular argument embarrassed me for a long time, because in the grand scheme of things, it was a waste of time and energy, and it was uncalled for on my end. My Cody was just being a gentleman.

I share all this to say that our relationship had its ups and downs, too. We were not perfect, but we were definitely perfect for each other.

My all-time favorite memories of us were always doing what he loved to do. I loved going fishing with him. Smelling like dirt, worms, and fishy water was well worth it when witnessing the joy in his soul. We didn't have to catch a single fish all day long, but I knew that time spent together meant absolutely every-thing to him and therefore it warmed my insides, too. I always cherished the cold, freezing mornings spent sitting high up in a deer stand or out in the middle of the woods somewhere, because it left him with the biggest smile the rest of the day. The woods would often be naked of wildlife and we wouldn't see a single creature all day long, but that time was priceless because he was by my side. I looked forward to giggling when one of us would fall asleep in the deer stand or have to suddenly use the restroom with no place to go. Lucky him for being born a male! When there were exciting times and we were able to claim our game and bring it home to harvest, it left him with many stories to run back and share with his friends.

Listening to him speak so proudly of me meant everything. I know it pleased him to have a mate willing and eager to do what he loved to do. I sought peace and comfort in finding someone in this great big world who enjoyed and cherished being outdoors like I do. Four-wheel riding, spending long nights sitting under the stars, and hiking unfamiliar trails together left engraved memories that will ignite passion in me for many years to come. I loved his sweet yet sour scent after doing those activities together. It was the scent of true love.

Throughout the course of our time together, we would witness couples boasting about how much they enjoyed and needed the space away from their spouses. But not us. We did not want the separation, we wanted to be near one another. He turned down many guys nights out of wanting to spend quality time with me, while I often told my girls "no thanks," looking forward to curling up next to him instead. Some couples teased us that it was unhealthy for us to spend so much time together, but we didn't mind the other's company. We often worked from home together at the same kitchen table that served as our office. And multiple times a week, when we went out to work, we served as the other's road dog. We had conversations in the past that sometimes it felt like we were craving or had withdrawals if we were apart from the other for too long. He dreaded work trips, and I didn't look forward to family vacations, if it meant the other wasn't coming with.

No matter how often I was with him, his presence always made my heart do somersaults. And no matter how much time in our relationship had passed, when he would speak, my tummy would flutter with butterflies. His delicate touch made all the fine hairs on my body rise up and salute the sun. Everything about him was captivating to me. Some couldn't see how we possibly got anything done in the company of the other. Some thought we needed to come up out of the water for air, but it's safe to say we didn't mind drowning as long as it was with each other.

After we were engaged to be married, Cody opened up to me about his point of view on the day we met on the track at Greenwood High School. He vividly remembered a glow about me that he couldn't quite put his finger on at the time. He said there was something about my aura I was radiating, even though he couldn't quite see me yet. He was led to go investigate the woman shining from across the track. He told me that ever since our initial meeting, he knew I would someday be his bride, but he just didn't know the details of how that would play out.

Ironically enough, a couple days after our very first date, I told my dad that I had met my future husband. My dad was shocked, to say the least, for no one knew I had even gone on a date with someone.

"Woah, woah, woah, Jack! Slow it down!" my dad said.

He sounded disappointed with my rather bold statement. But I *knew*, too, deep down it was the truth.

With a love this intense, it was hard to not put my spouse on a pedestal because he was such a *good* man! I was in awe of the light Jesus gave him while on this earth. His actions and responses to life were not of this world. His thankfulness and ability to see the positivity even during his darkest days was impeccable. I remember several occasions during our cancer journey when his thought process blew my mind and humbled my own heart.

One time, we were being discharged from Vanderbilt after a weekend stay. I was beyond stressed out and wrecked over Cody's depleting health condition. As the nurse was pushing my husband out towards the car in a wheelchair, Cody looked around analyzing the other families standing around. We saw a young man who had only one leg, an elderly woman who carried misery and bitterness all over her being, while another family was mourning over losing a loved one.

When the nurse was helping me get him into the car, she gave her best wishes to Cody and me through many warm encouraging words. While looking at the people around us, Cody told our nurse right then and there, "Don't be sad for me. It could always be worse, you know?" Even though I wasn't insensitive to the families around us, I also hadn't been thinking *that* way either. Cody realized something far greater than the flesh wanted to at times.

Another vivid memory also took place at Vanderbilt. Cody needed to get swabbed for yet again another COVID-19 test in order to be admitted into the hospital for an overnight stay. I had stopped counting after his eighth swab, but he'd had maybe twice that many, all in all. He was getting tested so many times that nosebleeds became inevitable. My heart ached for him. This time in particular, after already receiving the swab from both nostrils, his test came back "unreadable." That nurse and I were very upset that Cody would have to reswab all over again.

It just wasn't fair. I was not happy about this, and I made sure to let the entire medical team know of my frustrations as well. I hated seeing my husband get those darn tests. I hated watching him go through all of this, period! Yet Cody interrupted both of us by saying, "At least the test didn't read positive." Again, he stopped me in my tracks. He was right. I was thankful the Lord gave him incredible insight and a peaceful perspective.

Needless to say, for a long time, my human standards couldn't comprehend a greater love. My being would sink a thousand times into admiration for my mate when we would pray together. I can't recall him expressing a single prayer in which he asked God for anything for himself. Every conversation he spoke aloud to our Father that I witnessed, he would ultimately pray for others, even though he had a perfectly good excuse to ask for healing for himself.

He was the most selfless person I had ever known. Can you blame me if I idolized my husband, which is a normal spouse thing to do? Yet God tells us that we're supposed to love Him above all things. Jesus and the good Samaritan had a conversation about this topic in Luke 10:26–28. "Jesus said to the good Samaritan, 'What is written in the Law? How do you read it?' And he answered, 'You shall love the Lord your God with all your heart and with all your soul and with all your strength and with all your mind, and your neighbor as yourself.' And Jesus replied, 'You have answered correctly. Do this, and you will live.'"

Paul also reminds us in 1 Corinthians 11:3, "But I want you to understand that the head of every man is Christ, the head of a wife is her husband, and the head of Christ is God."

Our love for each other was out of this world and so deeply rooted from the start. It was as if instantly, both of us had felt a powerful force indicating that we were supposed to be together. As if the universe knew something neither of us did. But even though I knew our love came from God, before my husband's passing, I put him at the Lord's level, simply because he was in my sight and standing before me. I could physically see him and engage with him. I could hold him and know him, and it was *easy*.

But it's crystal clear to me now that I can and do love God more, despite the incomprehensibility of His love, because Cody is with Him now, and I've experienced loving him more now than ever. They are somewhere I cannot visually see with my earthly eyes, and they are somewhere I cannot physically touch with the human flesh. Yet I love them. Cody is merely an extension of the Father's love for me, and because I am of this world, I couldn't fully understand until after he left it. The only reason Cody even came into my life was because Christ saw it fit. Losing my husband has magnified the love I have for my Father. I not only love Cody far more than I ever did before, but Christ, too.

chapter nineteen

Hospice

This is an excerpt from my journal that was written on October 3, 2020, at 7:00 a.m.

I am running on maybe three hours of sleep here. Sometimes I'm afraid to close my eyes out of fear that when I wake up, my love won't be waking up with me. However, the exhaustion is still all worth it to bring glory to the Kingdom. He gives me strength to pull myself together effortlessly and get done what's needed to get done. His Spirit inside of me is alive, and it roars.

Cody was up all night stirring up a commotion. He kept wanting to walk around the room, go to the restroom, get a drink, mutter sounds, doze at my phone screen, which was reading scriptures aloud, and deeply analyze a sacred shawl that his childhood pastor had dropped off here. I had not seen this much energy out of him in weeks!

I needed a shower. I've been told that I stink and sadly I know. When you can smell yourself, haven't used real toothpaste in six days, and just got peed on by the man you love more than life itself, it starts to break you down. It's been extremely hard to leave his side to take a minute for myself, even if it is only for a few moments. I never want to leave his side. Never. Ever. EVER!

Reluctantly, I went ahead and hopped in the shower as soon as I knew he was in a deep sleep. The time was somewhere around 5:00 a.m., but who knows? Time doesn't seem to make sense to me anymore. I am mentally exhausted and fried. I've probably been like this for a while now, but the adrenaline seems to keep me going just fine. My husband is very well worth my final breath.

Not wanting to wake my love, I didn't bother with turning on the bathroom lights. Instead, the flashlight on my phone served just fine. He got overly stimulated and beyond overwhelmed yesterday by the ambulance ride and loving chaos that I didn't want to risk waking him from his much-needed sleep. He has been quite restless, yet oh so blessed.

God's presence follows me into the water. I felt so warm and free. And there I was. With Him. My first love! Praising, praying, reflecting. Thanking, thinking, crying. My bony body seemed fragile, frail, and not itself. I had burned my last ounce of stored fat days ago, yet this soul stands stronger than ever. Exhausted indeed but stirred in the Spirit. In the dark, yet not alone. We are blessed to see another beautiful day.

As I was deep in thought, I faintly began to hear what sounded like alarms going off on the other side of the bathroom door. It sounded like Cody's bedside equipment, except I remembered we don't have that anymore here at hospice. The more I tried to listen before jumping out to be right there, it sounded more like tinkling bells. Instantly, I began to worry. Maybe I had been in the shower too long and he needed me. My mom was staying the night with us, but maybe she needed me too. I tried to breathe and hurried to rinse the soap out of my hair, until the Spirit slowly started to convince me that mom would knock if it was something urgent. Then, I heard the noise again. Instead of freaking out this time, I remembered the night of August 17 when God spoke my name clear as day during my shower time. I instantly decided to mimic the actions and words of Samuel in the Bible this time. "Yes, Lord! Here I am, God. What do you need, Father?" I said aloud.

Silence.

So I resumed my shower in the dark, damp, and cold hospice bathroom. Once stepping out, I quickly dried off and threw on yet another one of my husband's oversized shirts and comfy sweat-pants. I was ready to see my Cody. I opened the door into the room, and there he was. He was still sleeping just as peacefully as I had left him. He didn't even budge a bit! Why was I worried? He was in the good hands of our peaceful Prince, being well taken care of getting the rest that he needed.

I am hearing you again, Jesus. What else should I do?

This next section blows my mind and gives me chills now. Christ led me to write this in my journal at 2:17 a.m. on October 4, while I had no clue my husband had only roughly fourteen hours left on this earth.

I'd like to think this is how God is responding—"Press into me and I'll do the rest. I'll give you my supernatural strength to seize each day. Don't give up on my ability to heal. My timing is perfect and it's only a matter of time. Let those from afar gather close to hear of this testimony and those near humble their hearts to pray without ceasing. Keep being you, my daughter—you're doing great!"

Modern-day language . . . *WOAH!* It's safe to say those words flowed straight through me from the Almighty. Not only did He know my heart, but He was preparing my heart for what was to come. Concluding my thoughts on the day of October 3, I continued . . .

Aside from yesterday morning being a bit rough due to the ammonia levels building up in Cody's liver, which was causing him more confusion, yesterday I laughed and smiled harder than I had in what seemed like a very long time. At first, Cody was unintentionally being rather stubborn with me and his best friend, Diante, who had flown in from Colorado to see him. He wanted to take out his IVs and go home, and nothing was convincing him of anything else. This made me very sad seeing him irritable and not in his right mind. For the first time ever, I could actually see the bright yellow jaundice when I looked into his eyes. I couldn't stare into them very long, because it brought tears to mine. These were not the same dark brown, chocolate eyes with a glossy, white exterior that I had fallen madly in love with. This shattered my heart into one thousand pieces. Seeing his glowing eyes made me afraid, but I didn't want Cody to see my doubt or despair.

After another horrible but brief vomiting episode, Cody was visited by his mom and two aunts who were extremely thankful to see him. This visit went great overall despite his mom having a snappy moment with me upon her arrival, but this was nothing the Lord didn't check her and have my back about. I was upset that she was steadily taking her frustrations and scared feelings out on me, when all I've been doing is caring for her son immensely. Being the people pleaser that I am, I wanted her approval again. I just want her to like and accept me.

Regardless of my own hurt, my favorite part of their visit was watching Cody be loved by his momma. Hugs and kisses, spoiling, and lots of sugar. She wanted to immerse him with care. There is something super special about a mother's love, even for a child at the age of thirty-six. It was obvious in that moment that she loved her firstborn baby boy more than anything. I was glad she came.

This cancer journey had brought out the best and worst of Eubanks' family flaws. Emotions were high and feelings were stepped on. I know deep down that everyone absolutely wanted what was best for Cody, but he said that this unnecessary feud hurt him more than the cancer did all day. I am beyond grateful that everyone put their best foot forward in front of him for this wonderful afternoon.

My mother-in-law and I prayed together over Cody's body for God to conduct complete healing and pump life back into his being. Our desires, wants, and wishes were easily brought before the Throne Room and laid at His feet. Doesn't Satan know that messing with a man's wife AND mother is a force to be reckoned with? Afterwards, we had a wonderful, much-needed talk in Cody's presence. She thanked me for caring for her son, and I thanked her for allowing and trusting me to do so.

I do not have any children, but my heart deeply goes out to her. If Cody were my son, I would not want to leave his side either, let alone watch another woman now have complete control over his health decisions. My heart rests well, knowing she trusts me with her most prized treasure. I know this can't be easy, but I appreciate it more than she will ever know.

After the family left, Cody and I received quality alone time for what seemed like the first time in a while. I'm not sure why, but it felt like I hadn't been alone with him in forever. He was all mine again and it felt good. Hubby was as alert as to be expected. I could see he was tired and super relaxed from the pain medicine, and astonishingly flirtatious. He couldn't keep his hands off of me. I could tell he missed me, too, by the way he pulled me close and by how grabby he had become. He was all for wanting his wife!

Nonetheless, we decided to spend this time together scrolling through memory lane on my camera roll, looking back at old photos of us. He kept surprising me by the way he remembered what we were doing in nearly every photo. I scrolled past one of my favorite photos of us from the honeymoon. He never approved of this photo because it was a wild, drunken night for us, and one could clearly tell!

"This one is one of my favorite photos together. Do you think this is a funny photo?" I asked.

"It is one of my favorites, too," he replied.

Really? Because he strongly disapproved of that one only months ago.

After showing him that photo, I clicked my phone to lock it off and put it in my back pocket. Cody looked at me in confusion. He extended his hand towards me like he was waiting for me to give him something.

"Well, aren't you going to take it?" he asked.

"Take what?" I said rather intrigued by his random question.

"A selfie of us," he answered.

In my head I thought, "Oh he's on a good one with this pain medication!" because he was never the selfie instigator. I pulled my phone back out, ready to capitalize on his request and positioned it to take a selfie of us. Click! It was a one-and-done, just to appease my husband. When I turned the phone around to look at the photo, I was shocked at what I saw. Cody's smile was huge! Babe really must have liked that because he was radiating.

"Look at that smile! I really miss that smile," I started to say. "You look great, but this is a terrible one of me."

He studied the photo with no energy left to recreate that gorgeous smile, but his words and actions were much better.

"My wife is sexy," he said as he grabbed me closer and began to kiss my neck and rub all over my back.

WHAT. My body felt like an electric current was running through it. I hadn't gotten time like this with him in several months. I totally submitted by letting him seduce the fire out of me. Is it wrong that I wanted to take my husband down in our hospice room?

There was no shame here and no doubt that I missed him in this way. I had been wearing the caretaker robe for so long now that being taken back to only his wife, partner, and lover was priceless and essential. I basked in the moment, allowing us to love on one another while fighting every urge to keep it PG. My heart and soul were overflowing and now a puddle on the floor that the nurse needed to come mop up.

Now pulling away from him, I needed a moment to gaze into his eyes. I knew he was going to be okay, because the flames were still burning bright.

Placing my palm on his forehead, I spoke aloud, "Cody, you are healed. I know it. Can you say that out loud for me?" I pleaded.

"I am healed," he whispered.

I asked him to repeat that three times and he did. I began to pray aloud with my hand still on his forehead, and I kid you not, whatever the Holy Ghost struck him with next scared me to bits. Cody stood up and insisted on going home. I tried to fight him back into the chair, but he was much larger and stronger than me. Cody darted for the door that led into the lobby, opened it, and stormed out.

As I was freaking out, watching and trying to stop my not-so-feeble-anymore husband from making a run for it, I yelled down the hall, "Help! Anyone, help! Nurses, help me!"

Two nurses got there in seconds and grabbed Cody from wandering any further.

When asked where he was going, his sharp response was "I am going home."

I was certainly shaking and in disbelief that this had just happened. The nurses and I burst into giggles before grabbing him a chair to sit in. None of us could believe that he had mustered up this kind of energy. Leave it to my Cody to bring laughter to us all without even trying.

chapter twenty

October 4, 2020

On this day in hospice, Cody had been mumbling in his sleep all night long. He would mutter constant jibber-jabber, and every so often he would throw my name into the mix, "Jackie." Without question, he was definitely having conversations with others from another realm. It was rather interesting to witness. Those who knew Cody knew he was a big talker and a huge bargainer. To this day, I joke that he was negotiating his way into heaven and up to something on my behalf and the behalf of his loved ones. If he were to leave this world, he wanted to ensure we were all properly taken care of. It was comforting for me to watch him sleep, because for the past couple of days he had been fighting sleep. His curiosity kept him awake. If I were to walk across the room, he would keep his eyes locked on me the entire time. He wasn't letting me out of his sight.

One of his aunts stayed the night with us at hospice. She was a huge, huge blessing to us both. For the first night in weeks, I slept like a baby while she pulled an all-nighter, making sure our Cody had everything he needed. We had one hiccup in the middle of the night when she abruptly awoke me, needing help with Cody. I bounced up eager to help my husband, while also feeling a bit guilty for falling into such a deep sleep. Thankfully, he only needed assistance in using the restroom. *Whew!* He did great and looked very good!

At dawn, I was able to wake up feeling rejuvenated, take a nice, refreshing shower, and easily pull myself together. It made a world of a difference getting that much-needed sleep. My heart rested well, knowing he was in good hands all night long.

When she and I reflected on the night, she shared with me how she enjoyed every bit of caring for her nephew and wouldn't have traded a single thing for that time with him. She enlightened me on every little detail throughout the night and did not miss a beat. She mentioned how Cody kept asking to "go home" like he had been doing since our arrival. The ammonia levels in his body were steadily rising, and it had caused him severe confusion at times. It was tough seeing him slower and disoriented, because healthy Cody was as sharp as a tack.

Once she left, Cody remained in this unconscious, muttering trance. The nurses assured me that he could still hear everything around him. They encouraged me by saying that he still wanted to hear the sound of my voice, but he was experiencing a mild coma that he would surely come out of at any time.

In the meantime, we attended Living Hope's 8:00 a.m. church service via online. Cody was still leaning back, resting in his recliner, so I propped my phone up on a pillow in his lap while I sat on the hospital bed beside him. I held his hand and didn't let go.

Christ has always spoken to me deeply through music, so I couldn't help but notice that all three worship songs sung that day proclaimed miracles and healing. I even screenshotted the choruses to each song because they spoke straight to my soul. This was more confirmation to me that Cody would beat the cancer.

- "Even The Impossible" Mack Brock

- "Over All I Know" Vertical Worship

- "Run to the Father" Cody Carnes

When I heard those songs, I believed that Cody was healed! You couldn't have convinced me of anything different. I just knew Cody was healed! My faith in *this* was astronomical. Everyone who came by to visit and also the nursing staff could noticeably see the tumor in his belly shrinking the past couple of days. The doctor tried to warn me that the cancer was spreading rapidly and was being absorbed into other parts of his body, but I didn't believe him. He was giving me a worldly answer, but I knew that the God I serve is bigger! Cody was starting to eat and drink a bit more, he was way more alert than his time in the hospital, and his skin was *glowing*. I didn't for a second believe he was getting worse. Cody Keon Eubanks was healed!

After church concluded, I simply stared at him while listening closely, attempting to make out his gibberish. I could have sat with him in that moment forever. I remember being so damn proud of him and in awe of every aspect of his being. He inspired me like none other, and the way he conducted himself not only through this trial but always was admirable. I am blessed to have been in his presence, not only on that day, but for the previous few years. Thankfulness was flooding my soul for this man.

Suddenly, the phone rang. It was Rita, an elder whom we both knew from Freedom, the Christian group I had attended when I got my first Bible. She insisted that she see us at once. And she was already standing outside of the hospice building. Honestly, I wasn't in the mood to entertain anyone, and there had been so many visitors in and out that the peace was enjoyable. But something deeper than me allowed for her to come on in. It was nice to see Rita on this day. She brought a peaceful, calm, and enhancing vibe. Her energy was alluring, and her words were beautiful. She prayed over us, laughed and cried with me, and listened to our story. Lord knows she was meant to be there in that moment. We enjoyably listened to Cody's mumbling together. We both smiled knowing exactly whom he was communicating with. God Almighty, of course.

After another prayer, Rita began to talk to Cody. I don't remember her exact words, but she told him that God was still good. She encouraged him to lean into Christ and praise Him. Whatever she said was powerful indeed, because the most magical, beautiful, tremendously captivating thing happened next. My beloved husband, still in this unconscious state, lifted his hands in the air and reached for the stars. His arms were shaking from being weak, yet he kept them raised high in the air for as long as he could. He was worshiping our Father! And it was evident. His glow while doing this was exceedingly beautiful. He was *still* giving God the glory. Certainly the smile on my face could have been seen from anywhere on earth. *I love you, Cody. I love you, Jesus.*

When his hands finally dropped, his whole demeanor instantly changed. Cody became quickly agitated and attempted to lift himself out of the recliner. Still not able to communicate words, he attempted to stand up on his own, but he couldn't muster up the strength. Rita nor I had the muscle to support his dead weight, so I pressed the call light for help. As soon as the nurses came in, chaos struck. Everything happened so suddenly. Rita sensed that it was best for her to leave, because the nurses felt like he was trying to relieve himself. Unfortunately with him not being able to lift himself up in that moment and still going in and out of consciousness, the nurses thought it best that it was time to insert a catheter.

Two nurses and I carefully transferred him from the recliner to the bed. My heart was racing, and my palms were sweaty by the commotion going on within this room. They rapidly undressed him to bare nakedness. My head was spinning so fast, yet instinct had kicked in for me to be strong and help the nurses with whatever they said my husband needed. Naturally, Cody wasn't cooperating with the nurses regarding inserting the catheter. He was fighting them with all of his might. Even with him being weak, his size and uncontrollable strength was still great compared to the three of us little women.

One nurse asked me if I would hold him down and attempt to soothe him so that they could get the catheter inserted. My heart had physically broken at this thought. I couldn't believe she was literally asking me to pin him down while they inflicted pain to his gentleman downstairs. It felt like a kick to the gut. I would have rather shot my own foot. I wanted to instantly snap back at her with an evil *HELL NO*, but my desire for Cody to feel better won out.

I felt excruciating pain in my heart while holding his chest down for this process. I couldn't bear to look, so I buried my face into his shoulder and closed my eyes. I attempted to comfort him by telling him that it was all going to be okay and this would help him feel better. He still couldn't speak words, but his loud grunting and moans told all I needed to hear. When they were done, I instantly begged him for his forgiveness.

"Babe, I am so sorry," I repeated over and over again in his ear.

I assumed that this was the worst to come, because his body became extremely still. Shortly after, the muttering and gibberish started to resume, and he looked peaceful again. My heart was oh so broken.

During this exceedingly traumatizing event going on inside, we could hear a commotion beginning to build up outside. No one knew what was going on in between our four walls besides Cody, the nurses, and myself, but my mother had already made arrangements for her Bible study group to gather on the back patio, to spend time in prayer over us. It was a lovely sentiment, and the kindness was appreciated. Once things calmed down inside, the wife of our dear family friend who had married us opened the back door to deliver two communion cups. Within seconds she was able to hand them to me before the nurse shoved her out. I agreed that now wasn't the time for visitors. I could not breathe and was a wreck by what had just happened to my better half.

Within a few more minutes, the nurses had left, and the hospice doctor came into our room. I had grown quite fond of this man. It was seemingly evident that he cared about Cody and me. His gentle nature was pacifying, yet everything was so surreal. With sorrow-filled eyes, he looked at me while explaining the stages of death he believed my husband was now entering. He told me that my love would not be waking up anymore. His voice trembled while telling me to say my final goodbyes and to call anyone who might wish to say theirs as well. Anything else he might've said was bypassed due to the overwhelming deluge on my mental capacity.

As soon as he left and shut the door behind him, I wept. Nothing seemed real. The nightmare I had been living had to be coming to an end, because I was drowning. I had always heard growing up that if you die in a dream, you don't wake back up. I was dying, so surely waking up was coming soon, and if not, I would soon be face to face with Jesus Christ. My heartbreak in being potentially separated from Cody was undeniable. My sobs were out of control, and I was running out of H20 in my body. It wasn't until my faithful God pulled me back into the game, that I knew I had to remember what He was telling me. I had to remember His promises.

I grabbed one of the two communion cups filled with some type of grape juice and a thin chip from the nightstand beside us. I prayed and thanked God aloud for my husband and our faith in Him. Once opening the cup, I acknowledged that we would be receiving these elements for the nourishment of our minds, bodies, and spirits. Cody and I were *one,* bonded by a holy marriage. So only taking one through my mouth seemed feasible. Afterwards, I grabbed the anointed ChapStick that was sitting on the back of the headboard and blessed our lips. I reminded Cody, again, that if the Lord was calling him home to heaven, he couldn't refuse that beautiful offer for the sake of me. I would be okay. He had my blessing and full permission to go home to Jesus.

Once this sacred moment between the Lord, my husband, and myself was over, I called Cody's mother. I slowly explained to her what the doctors had told me, and that she needed to get here immediately. But she told me she would not be coming to his bedside. And this broke my heart even more. Yet instead of reacting with rage like I wanted to do, I quickly realized that her absense was between her and the Lord. So I hung up.

Falling back into an immense devastation, I don't even remember sending out texts to several of our close friends, and the greatest prayer warriors that we knew, to come immediately. I felt as if he would be raised up from that bed if enough believers believed. He was going to walk again. I knew it! I couldn't comprehend anything different. Later, he would indeed be raised and walk again, just not how my flesh had envisioned.

Before I could even blink or gather my thoughts, the room became packed with people. Cody was truly a fisher of men. Our room was swarmed with men and women, short people and tall people, round people and thin people, black people, white people, and people in between those skin tones. We had Christians and Atheists, Democrats and Republicans, joyful people and depressed people, millionaires and people struggling to pay their water bills—all in our presence. At this moment, everyone was longing for one thing, our Cody, while heaven was rejoicing at the works he had done in bringing all of God's children together in harmony.

Some of our friends were praying and singing, while others were crying and laughing. Some were sharing stories of the past, and others were enlightening us about the future. The English tongue was spoken aloud along with other prayer languages. Some people felt comforted by the atmosphere being created and the thought of Cody being face to face with Jesus, while others were filled with fear of the unknown. Not everyone's relationship with the Lord was being expressed the same. And it was all beautiful. Some people attempted to cast judgment among others, but thankfully God kept the differences in that room at bay. Who knew Satan would try to come in and disrupt such a glorious day!

People offered comforting words to us both by saying they would look after me when he was gone. We all pitched in expressing our love, thanks, and well wishes to Cody—my husband, our friend, our brother. We all wanted him to hear us and know how much he meant to us. Some told him about the impact he had made in each of our lives. We prayed, begged, and pleaded for him not to suffer, yet we longed for him to stay with us forever. In my opinion, God was extremely pleased by the love that overflowed and filled the room.

My eyes rarely left my husband's face. I was called to be Cody's helper and mate until death did us part. My body was suctioned to and paralyzed by his side. The nurse had given me pineapple juice and a sponge to soak his lips and keep his mouth from getting too dry. If only I could've breathed life back into him. The voices and commotion behind me didn't faze me one bit, because all I could feel was the presence of God. I felt his *healing* would arrive at any moment.

At one point the room grew quiet. All that could be heard was sniffling and weeping. I felt the Spirit nudge me to shake up the room for His glory. Even though I don't have the greatest voice on the planet, Cody always loved when I would sing for him. Sometimes I would randomly send him an audio clip of me singing in the car, and it would make his day! So I began to sing one last song for my husband. I began to sing "Way Maker."

"Way Maker" by Leeland has always been my favorite worship song. We often sang and danced to it together on full blast, but it means so much more to me now than it ever did before. So bittersweet. I sang this for my husband right before he got called home to heaven. He was going home to be with Jesus, but my flesh desperately ached for him to stay here on earth.

Up until that moment, I *still* wasn't fully convinced he was dying. Just the day before, he was seducing the fire out of his bride and running up the hallway to escape. The Lord kept endlessly sprinkling me with hope that he was getting better. Those close to us were worried I was in denial throughout this entire journey, but I was simply being blessed with an indescribable amount of faith that he would *live*. God was showing me that he *was* getting better. Cody would live and be healed, just not physically here with me.

The uncontrollable desire I had to interject the cancer into my own body was infuriating. I wanted so badly to take the suffering away from him. He didn't deserve the pain he had been dealt those past four months or so. My thoughts had been everywhere at all times since the initial diagnosis, but especially in those moments. I was crying out to my Savior in despair.

Why him, God? You need him here spreading Your message and being an example to others. Let him keep going because he makes this world a much better place. He is so undeserving, and this couldn't be happening to a kinder or more loving guy. People need to see his bright light and experience his deep love. He has so much more to see and do for You in this life. Give the cancer and agony to me, Lord. Take me instead. Let him live! Perform a miracle like only You can. God, I know You can do this, and I know that You will.

Faith the size of a mustard seed was all I needed, right? Well, I had *pounds* of it. I took Cody's hand and repetitively spoke the words and actions of Jesus in John 5: "Pick up your mat and walk. Rise, Cody. You are healed. Sit up and talk to me, love." I always remembered what Jesus spoke in Matthew 7:7: "Ask, and it will be given to you; seek, and you will find; knock, and it will be opened for you." And Mark 11:24: "Therefore I tell you, whatever you ask in prayer, believe that you have received it and it will be yours." Cody wasn't dying that day. I had too much confidence that he would be *healed*.

More moments passed until the heat from numerous bodies cleared the room. Someone had been patting the back of my neck with a cold rag due to my body burning from the inside out. I didn't even feel hot. I didn't feel anything, actually. Once the room had somewhat emptied, someone yanked me away from my husband's side and changed my soaked sweatshirt to a comfy, light T-shirt. I couldn't tell you who helped with this transition, but all I longed for was to get back to my husband's flank.

At this point, the nurses had come back in and forced everyone to leave except for me and them. They were changing the sheets from his body naturally relaxing and releasing. They had expressed concerns a bit earlier, saying that his heart and body were still so strong, and they feared he would be suffering in this state for days, perhaps even a week. None of us wanted Cody to suffer and struggle, especially for that long, if going home to heaven was His will. Suddenly, as the nurses had rolled him over on his side, certain organs had collapsed, and blood rushed out of his orifices. I immensely regret having to see my husband, my best friend, my leader, my love, my life partner, my protector, my mate, my confidant, my better half, my soulmate, my Cody in this way. *This* was the turning point for me when the reality of my husband dying to this world became real.

As the nurses were rushing all around me to clean up my husband, all of a sudden the sliding door opened and his mom rushed in. It doesn't matter how or why, but a friend had called to get her there. Cody's mother came! I instantly panicked, hoping neither she nor the two family members she walked in with would see the image of him that I had just witnessed. It broke me, and I was hoping to save them from that sight, too. She ran over to Cody's right side, and I took my place on his left. She mourned and held her baby boy with so much distress. My heart ached for her. We put our arms around one another as we smothered into Cody. The three of us tangled together, holding each other strenuously for what felt like no time at all.

I remember wishing that the past few months had been this way, and we'd been all in sync with one another. No words could even begin to describe the grief in those moments. Within ten to fifteen minutes, maybe, there was no more heartbeat detected. He was with Jesus, the Prince of Peace.

♡ ♡ ♡

Writing about that moment now reminds me of one that happened a couple years earlier. Cody and I had been having breakfast, sitting in the living room at our old apartment. We were enjoying the beautiful morning along with each other's company when out of the blue, an agonizing cry filled the streets for what seemed like miles. It sounded like a wolf crying for the moon, but it had lost its howl. It was a deep bellowing that couldn't possibly have come from the human body. That shrieking wail pierced my ears so vastly that they stung. Cody jumped up immediately, asking, "What was that?" I'm not sure why or how, but in that moment I knew that the sound had come from the soul of my friend, Hope. Instinctively my exact response to my Cody was "It happened."

Dear friends and neighbors of ours had been fighting their own long, taxing cancer journey themselves, which went on for several years. Our hearts were torn, and our thoughts were always with them, but how could we have possibly related to their pain and suffering at the time? His wife wailed the deepest sorrow of a cry I had ever heard in my life when he took his last breath. For some strange reason, it resonated with me, and I never forgot *that* sound.

I made that sound the moment my other half's heart stopped beating. It was a roar I couldn't possibly recreate even if I tried. It physically hurt me to let it out, but it just came. And there was no holding back. I had never felt or experienced a burn so excruciating. A piece of me was gone, and I couldn't do anything but weep.

For the first time, I truly noticed how strained his body had become. When had I become so blind to what was happening to him? How did I not see what everyone else had been seeing for months? The hair on his head was longer than I had ever seen it before. His skin didn't have the warm glow that made him shine. His eyes that were a bit cracked open had lost their charm and twinkle. His once full cheeks were gone and divided by his thick cheekbones that were cutting through. His facial hair was much longer and curlier than normal. His lips were not the full, thick lips I had loved kissing for all those years. They were weak, cracked, and dry. The veins in his neck were soft to the touch. His chest was sucked in, and there was no muscle in his arms. His cold hands could not grab mine back, and his fingers wouldn't intertwine themselves with mine. I could see and feel his ribs instead of those fluffy love handles I had once loved grabbing. His pelvic bones were noticeably bony and piercing through his skin. The name he had given his friend was Johnson. And Johnson was not electric or excited to see me anymore. His thighs were flabby from the muscle in them having vanished. They normally would be able to crush bricks, but they looked so feeble. His calves had lost their power, and all that was left was mostly bone. Even his feet and toes had lost the puffiness from the swelling. The figure before me was not my Cody. My Cody had gone to heaven and left his shell behind.

In that moment, everything I had known and loved, including the magical future we had worked so hard to build together, was gone. A part of me died to this world. And then, at twenty-three years old, I was a widow, and Cody was with Jesus.

chapter twenty-one

Death Has Lost Its Sting

The moment my husband went to heaven, I couldn't feel. I couldn't feel my fingers or my toes, and I couldn't feel myself breathing in and breathing out. I couldn't feel anything, as our life together had literally flashed before my eyes. I couldn't even feel my mom rush into the room attempting to smother me with an enormous mama bear hug. She tried tugging and pulling to wrap me closer and closer, but her embrace wasn't enough to even slightly absorb the knife in my chest. The room was melting hot, and I wanted to get completely undressed, yet the room was freezing cold, and I wanted to bury myself deep underneath the covers. I couldn't emotionally or mentally grasp the mere fact that his soul was no longer connected to his physical, earthly body. Trying to retain my thoughts in that moment was impossible. Was I longing for him to come back to this dreadful place again with me, instead of being in heaven experiencing wholeness? Was I burdened with sorrow that I was now widowed on this earth? Was I replaying all of our good times or bad times over and over in my head? Was I relieved that his suffering was over? Was I wishing that I could turn back time? Was I glad that he was with Jesus? No telling what clouded the space in my head or my heart. I couldn't feel *anything.*

Again, in those initial moments after he passed, I couldn't tell you how I was feeling. One thing is for certain—after Cody's final breath on this earth, my eyes *opened.* In that moment, I unquestionably *knew* that the empty temple lying before me was not my husband. The effects of the sickness were revealed to me, and his being was unrecognizable. The body looked somewhat like him, but I knew it wasn't Cody. It was apparent that the substance of his soul had vanished to heaven and in front of me was a lifeless structure. In that moment, the Lord had given me a special gift despite the aching in my soul. He blanketed me with *peace that surpasses all understanding.*

Although I had shed tears from being physically separated from my beloved partner, God's sovereignty made pointing to Himself *effortless.* Unfortunately, losing my husband was my first time losing someone extremely close to me. I couldn't comprehend death before, or possibly begin to relate to others when they would lose a loved one. I could not have truly grasped their pain. I never understood how people could keep going and living or even smile again after someone they loved dearly passed away from this world. It never occurred to me that God gives His children strength to keep on keeping on. He allows those who press into Him to keep going with the knowledge that your loved one still lives on inside of you. The Lord made it to where those of us who seek Him will experience death with no sting! What even is death? Will we really even die?

I had been meditating and trying to put my finger on why my husband's passing didn't feel real, and why I felt closer to his spirit now more than ever before. Shouldn't he be gone, gone? But the answer I kept getting was, "No," which explains why I can still vividly seek, see, and feel his presence daily.

People seem to think I should be mad at God or something for taking my husband from me. How could I be mad? God didn't do this to my Cody. In fact, I've expressed the emotion of jealousy often towards God and Cody since his passing simply for leaving me here in this sick world. Not mad over him passing but because of my own envy of feeling left behind. Shamefully, I am jealous of Cody. He made it! He's where we all should aspire to be some day.

This journey has deeply made me realize that we are to enjoy this life we were given and live it to the fullest on mission for Jesus, but also rejoice and have peace in knowing it gets much better than this. Passing from this world is nothing to fear *if* you're right with Christ. He's said it and I'll say it again: this world is not our home! It really sucks right now with everything stirring up in the media. Politics, racial wars, sicknesses, natural disasters, arguments, hate, etc. = *ugghh! But God.* God has prepared a place much sweeter than this for us to go home to someday.

We thought Cody's physical presence here was strong and impactful, but his spiritual presence is so much thicker! To me, it feels like he never left. I am still seeing him move and work. I've witnessed him still give and love. Sure, the longing I have for him to be physically close to where I can actually see and hold him hurts like none other, but there's no hole in my heart. It's actually never felt so full. Society views death differently than Christ views it.

Jesus says, "Truly, truly, I say to you, whoever hears My word and believes Him who sent Me has eternal life. He does not come into judgment but has passed from death to life. Truly, truly, I say to you, an hour is coming, and is now here, when the dead will hear the voice of the Son of God, and those who hear will live" (John 5:24–25).

These are just two of MANY verses on how Jesus conquered death so that we, too, may live. On this earth we are dead and dying, but we will soon be alive with Him. This truth has made me smile, cry, and sing over and over—Cody is flourishing now more than ever. If I can recognize Christ's goodness and experience His love in my absolute lowest valley, surely you can, too.

It wasn't until I heard a sermon on December 13, 2020, that *this* dawned on me and truly sunk in. The preacher read 1 Corinthians 15:54–57:

> WHEN THE PERISHABLE PUTS ON THE IMPERISHABLE, AND THE MORALITY PUTS ON IMMORALITY, THEN SHALL COME TO PASS THE SAYING THAT IS WRITTEN:
>
> "DEATH IS SWALLOWED UP IN VICTORY." "O DEATH, WHERE IS YOUR VICTORY? O DEATH, WHERE IS YOUR STING?"
>
> THE STING OF DEATH IS SIN, AND THE POWER OF SIN IS THE LAW. BUT GIVE THANKS TO GOD, WHO GIVES US THE VICTORY THROUGH OUR LORD JESUS CHRIST.

He gave an example of how a father and son were riding in the car together with the windows rolled down. Suddenly, a bee flies in the car, and the young boy freaks out because he is allergic. The father extends his hand and catches the bee in his palm. He holds it for a while and then releases the bee inside the car. The boy begins to panic again, until the dad says, "Son, do not be afraid. The bee only has one stinger, and it is now in my hand. He can no longer hurt you. He can fly around in attempts to scare you and strike fear, but he cannot hurt you, because I have taken the stinger, so you won't have to."

Death has lost its sting because He who knew no sin became sin and took the punishment for me, for Cody, and for each of us. Christ took the stinger of death! It's seriously the power of God within my soul, masking the brokenness my flesh feels. My flesh wants nothing more than to open a wardrobe and escape to Narnia and never return. Me, myself, and I would love nothing more than to crawl up under the covers and never come out, *but our God.* The girl in the mirror is weak, exhausted, and afraid, but God has her back and will never lead her astray. He refuses to go a day without blessing me, but it's up to me to recognize and count the favors He gives. Some days these might be easier to spot than others, but I force myself to count those blessings despite the pain in my heart, because ultimately Jesus has control of my soul. He has filled a void in me that is purely *unexplainable.*

My entire perspective has changed. Worldly death no longer scares me because my King and my Cody await me on the other side. They alone make it a beautiful place. It's a rarity in and of itself that I can see the beauty in what is to come. There is more out there than just this broken world in which we temporarily live right now. And Cody and I *still* have a beautiful union. A bond and connection like that does not just fade away. Everything in our lives together happened on purpose to bring glory to the Kingdom.

Although I may not physically see Cody for a long time from now, that is okay. We will have much time to catch up, make new memories, and hang out in eternity together, side by side praising our Maker. The revelation in knowing this world is merely temporary compared to all of eternity brings me great joy! It gets much better than this, friends.

chapter twenty-two

One Day Gone

Our home had been full of family and friends flowing in and out while we were housed at the hospital and hospice. So essentially, I didn't go straight home to an empty house. Although there were several warm bodies surrounding me, none of them were whom I desired to see the most. Our house didn't feel like a home anymore.

I felt like everything had been only a dream that a good night's sleep would surely help me recover from. Apparently, a couple of people tried waking me up later on in the night to check on me, but I was out like a light. Not even a horn to the ear could have broken the deep level of sleep I had fallen into. My mom had also taken my phone into another room sometime in the midst of the night, fearing it would eventually wake me by its constant ringing, vibrations, and lights. Everyone was reaching out to give their condolences, but I was out cold to the world.

Although I got a solid night's sleep from severe exhaustion and mental strain, the next day I was solely numb from shock. Though part of me had already been granted with peace, calmness, and stillness that my partner was no longer suffering in agony, I still wept. I was in full-on processing mode about the entire journey I had just gone through. Was everything truly over, just like that?

In the morning, I started my first day of my new reality locked away in my room on my knees before a picture of me and my precious Cody, crying out to heaven. Even though I couldn't see Cody, I could feel him with me more than ever before. I could feel his soul closer than ever to my own. I could feel his spirit hugging me while wiping away the tears on my cheeks. I could hear his voice assuring me that he was happy, safe, and in no more pain. I could hear his deep voice confidently telling me that he would still never ever leave me.

Despite the loss of a lifetime, I felt blessed in those moments. I *still* feel blessed. The warm sun was shining and beaming bright through my bedroom window for confirmation. The Spirit sent me into a state of praise and thanksgiving. I felt honored to have been given this bond with Cody, and I treasured the time we got to spend together. It was evident that I needed him, and he needed me, too. I was granted the privilege of marrying the most wonderful human, and he was insanely crazy about me. He would have found a way to hang the moon for me if I had asked. In that moment, and for many to come, I had no choice but to smile and reminisce on our joyful times and milestones we had overcome together.

Pulling myself together, I walked into the living room only to find a group of my family and friends who love me, waiting to spoil and embrace me with whatever I may have needed. And with all the love overwhelming me and multiple ears waiting to hear how I was, I only longed to share my new revelations with my mentor. So I called her over and we escaped into privacy. Although I don't remember our conversation in its entirety, she helped me process and fill in the gaps of what I was trying to convey.

Cody isn't dead. He didn't leave us and never will. Someday "... I shall go to him, but he will not return to me" (2 Samuel 12:23).

Here was my tribute on Facebook, one day after my husband left this earth:

> Sunday, October 4th around a quarter to 4:00 pm, this world got a bit darker. Heaven rejoiced as they welcomed my beloved husband & best friend into eternity. "For this world is not our home, we are looking forward to our everlasting home in heaven." —Hebrews 13:14

Cody was truly a fisher of men. He brought together everyone from everywhere. The Throne Room was highly glorified at the time of his passing with people of different spiritual levels, skin colors, political views, financial statuses, etc., leaning on one thing—our Maker to bless our Cody. We are made to love, and Cody displayed this perfectly. "This is my commandment, that you love one another as I have loved you." —JOHN 15:12

His legacy lives on. I have been slowly writing a book by documenting the days since this journey began for us, hoping it would be the earthly ending that I/we all wanted. My flesh, our flesh, and this world is shattered and crushed at why, but we have this to stand on: "Jesus answered them, 'What I am doing you do not understand now, but afterwards you will understand.'" —JOHN 13:7

After much prayer, I will continue to honor God & my Cody and finish their book. Please stay tuned.

I pray this over each of you that the Lord fills you with peace far past your human understanding. "And the peace of God, which surpasses all understanding, will guard your hearts and your minds in Christ Jesus." —PHILIPPIANS 4:7

I thought I knew God well before this trial, but He has pursued mine & Cody's heart endlessly & vigorously each day. The true miracle is being face to face with Jesus and we never lost the faith. I don't know what comes next right now and that's okay.

As of now there will be a Celebration of Life for Cody like he wanted this Wednesday, October 7th from 12–6pm at the Cason's Cove Venue farm where we got married—and ALL are welcome. Come & go as you please, stay as long as you'd like, social distance, bring lawn chairs, blankets, & food, wear face masks inside, and share many laughs, cries & stories, and BYOB-Bring your own BALLOON for releasing.

Cody, I will always love you. Xoxo

—*Jackie*

Later in the day, my mom and older sister drove me to the funeral home. Going there was the part I was absolutely dreading the most. How was anyone supposed to rush to make such wretched decisions about their loved ones? How was a young woman supposed to bury her new husband? How was I supposed to give my Cody a "goodbye"? I just didn't understand, nor did my spirit receive anything well for that matter. I refused to say "goodbye," because it wasn't goodbye. I was so confused as to why the world was making me think or feel otherwise.

During the duration of that car ride, I prayed for confidence and certainty to the best of my ability to keep honoring Cody and to make Christ proud. But I was paralyzed. It wasn't until the exact moment in which we pulled into the parking lot of Burnam & Son Mortuary, and put the car into park, that the Holy Spirit intervened. His presence was exceedingly felt.

One of my favorite songs, "Oceans" by Hillsong United, came on the radio. I insisted on turning the volume all the way up, and all of us were heavily drawn in by Him through the lyrics sung by this band. It was confirmed that Jesus and Cody were on each side of me, holding my hands.

The only explanation for his celebration of life coming together and falling perfectly into place was God. After much brainstorming on what we should do to honor him for our memorial, a phone call from the owner of Cason's Cove unexpectedly came in. Out of the blue, she offered us the date they had available if we wanted to host this event there. After calling to discuss and get opinions on the arrangements with his family, we confirmed that this was the right thing to do. Before Cody passed, in my notebook I had asked him, "What was the best day of your life?" His response was "Getting married." This was the best day of my life, too. Celebrating his life overall in a place where we had spent our best day seemed brilliant. My family and our friends took the vision I had in making his day great and worked hard to make it *extraordinary*! We all knew it was exactly what Cody would have wanted.

As much as I longed to take all illness away from my husband, Cody wouldn't have let me or anyone else carry what he preserved as his destiny. Plus, now speaking, who was I to rob his calling for eternal life? Cody did suffer short term here, but now he dances in heaven with no distress. For now, we are to face far more hardships until Christ calls us home, too.

In my eyes, if at least one person could be drawn closer to Christ from our journey, pushing forward in faith was what I needed to do. Cody told me to be strong and keep going, so I had to remember just that. Since he was so courageous, I knew I could be, too. The Lord was showing me that our journey together—the three of us—was only the beginning.

chapter twenty-three

4:44

This is an excerpt from my journal that was written on October 9, 2020, at 4:44 a.m.

I just had a dream of my precious Cody. Simple yet oh so sweet. The spiritual aspect radiates and is filling our bedroom as I type. It was a dream of his face. I felt his presence drastically all around my body. I know and feel him watching and protecting me while I sleep. I've been sleeping with the stuffed bear he gave me this past Valentine's Day more now than before. Every time I wake up, I'm squeezing its neck. In the dream he was smiling, yet a tear was rolling down his cheek. Anyone who knows Cody knows that he is the most mentally sound person ever. Cody hardly ever cried.

I have only seen my husband cry three times. The first time I saw him cry was on our wedding day. As I walked down the aisle a stream of crocodile tears were consuming his face. He was attempting to wipe them away but couldn't soak them up with his sleeve fast enough. By the time I got to the arch, he was standing in a puddle. All who were there saw a side of him that I was experiencing for the first time, too. I couldn't help but smile ear to ear, knowing I had found my soulmate. It was beautiful.

My second time seeing him cry was at church. After his diagnosis, his mentor invited us to start sitting with him and his family. Cody sat down in the pew, looked around for a bit, engaged in conversation, and shortly got up and ran to the hallway. I freaked out and rushed after him, knowing he had been throwing up so much lately. I thought he was heading to the restroom, but when I caught up with him, he just needed a minute to collect himself. I didn't understand why at the time, but after church he told me the love was too overwhelming for him at that moment. He was blessed to be in his Father's house, sitting next to his wife and a family whom we look up to and aspired to be like very much.

And this was my third time seeing him cry.

I'll never forget what Cody told me one of our last days in the hospital . . . It was one of the worst nights of my life. He couldn't eat, sleep, pee, poop, walk, or hold anything down. My shirt had his blood all over it, and I was not okay. He was miserable. The constipation was putting so much pressure on his belly, and he was in so much pain. Cody was holding my hand while attempting to use the bedside commode. He squeezed my hand tight, and I heard a little sniffle. He looked up at me with tears in his eyes.

My heart aching said something like this, "Oh Cody, it's okay to cry. Let it out. You've been so strong. You don't have to be strong anymore. You deserve to cry. Babe, let it out." Cody, still coaching me in this dark moment, looked up at me and said, "Sometimes showing your weakness is your biggest strength."

This man was unlike anyone I had ever met before. He could have acted, said, or done anything he wanted in this low valley, but he still remained composed and chose to stay as positive as he could. He never lost faith. His peace about the situation surpassed all understanding and his spirit passed this gift along to me. If I can be a fraction of the person Cody was on his worst days in my best days, I'll be doing just fine.

I've decided that the number four is Cody's number. His life began and ended on a four in three different ways. Cody was born on December 4, 1983, and he passed on October 4, 2020, around a quarter to 4:00 p.m. Ever since he went to heaven, I find myself searching and paying more attention to this number. It wasn't a coincidence that I was woken up at 4:44 a.m. today on October 9, 2020, to record this dream.

chapter twenty-four

Grieving Is Inevitable

This is an excerpt from my journal that was written on January 13, 2021, at 9:27 p.m. I've added this entry to expose the human nature of grieving.

Sometimes I wake up and my mind is running faster than my body. I beg God to give me the strength to heave myself out of bed. Other mornings my body has too much spunk, and my mind cannot possibly keep up. It's always a rat race between mind, body, flesh, and soul. Sometimes I feel ready to conquer a day, and everything seems to be in sync. I really look forward to those good days and fully embrace them when they come. The supernatural joy that intercedes fills the gaps of my fleshly devastation. It allows me to see this situation for what it truly is: a secret weapon from Yours Truly—Jesus!

Occasionally though, I'll weep coming home to our big, empty house without him trailing me through the threshold. I miss those dreamy big, brown, and beautiful eyes, and how they would stare in admiration straight to my soul. He saw me for who I truly am and respected me by putting Christ before himself. He viewed me as a daughter of the King.

Nowadays, confrontation, pointless gossip, and drama tend to wear me out more than normal. I could hardly stand it before, but now I can't entertain it at all. Everything else seems so minuscule compared to the heartbreak I'm enduring. Lately, it's been hard for me to listen to friends when they complain about their love lives, or other issues in their day-to-day lives. Don't they know I'd do anything to have my partner back? I wish they'd realize my mental state is fried. However, most of the time I completely zone out or I choose to avoid it altogether. Life is too short to be consumed by the negative.

I try to express how I feel sometimes to friends who seem to know me like they know the back of their hand, but so much doesn't seem to stick or resonate with them. And how could it? Am I too hard on them? Perhaps I am expecting too much out of those who have no clue? If only someone understood. Even other widows who have been through similar heartbreak seem unrelatable, because each person handles their pain differently.

I do have regrets of entertaining the meaningless arguments between me and my mate that wasted our precious time together. I've sat at the foot of his recliner, picturing him still resting there.

My hand often wanders in the middle of the night, searching for his body to pull myself close, but his body's warmth can no longer be found. I often catch myself talking to Cody as if he were right next to me. I talk aloud daily, hoping he'll give me vivid signs. A voice from the clouds shouting back to me clear as day, "I love you. I am proud of you. Keep going, my girl!" would be super nice. I know that he's still so proud of me now even during my darkest days, but I wish to hear his voice say it aloud. I know he would have understood and been able to comfort me better than anyone else.

Shamefully, sometimes it bothers me that others who say they miss him still get to go home to their spouses, children, and families. They get to run back to their careers, life accomplishments, and goals as if nothing ever happened. Where were many of them when he was ill? I was the only person one could always find at his side. I was the one person who always held his hand during the darkest of nights. Others could run home and forget that ache in the pit of their stomach for at least a little bit, while I've been left behind, still soaking it all in. Everyone else's world gets to keep moving forward while mine is paused and consumed in our past and what I thought was supposed to be our future. Our future got swept away during the high tide waves and washed out to sea, never to resurface again. I'd imagine it's easy to point fingers at what I'm doing now when others still have someone or something to go home to. Cody was my home.

Although I've been told that as time passes my mindset won't be solely focused on him anymore, I would like to think that he will resonate with me forever. We spent every day together and slept next to one another each night. We were each other's good morning and goodnight. We knew each other on a deeper scale than anyone else. We were two peas in a pod and very best friends. We were one another's first pick, cuddle mate, thunder buddy, accountability partner, and secure confidant. We shared secrets together from the rest of the world. He had my back, and I had his. As loyal spouses we were intimately intertwined on the deepest of levels. We were one.

There's no sugarcoating the fact that grieving sucks. It's like someone pitched you a wicked curveball you never saw coming. You went to swing at it, but you totally missed and got yourself unbalanced. In fact, it drilled you in the face! You're expecting one thing, but you're given another. In my situation, I knew receiving that ball of my husband passing away was a possibility (a possibility I honestly never thought would happen), but the aftermath was something I couldn't possibly have prepared for. I'd imagine it's also similar to a movie in which someone takes an unfamiliar turn and never finds their way back home. Ultimately, they must figure out how to survive at their new destination no matter the obstacles they face or the lack of supplies they have. If I am being brutally honest, sometimes it feels like I am constantly being strangled, but I cannot break free or escape the harshness of the grip.

According to much research and many conversations I've had, grieving the loss of a close loved one is by far the most uncertain transition in life. One strives to bounce back from it, but truly never recovers. It's always uncharted territory. You can have all the peace in the world and perhaps move forward with life, but the longing and closeness to that person will always still linger. Grieving is inevitable.

When I reflect on the day my husband passed, it all seems so beautiful and peaceful to me, but those weren't necessarily my thoughts at the time. In those moments, I was waiting for an earthly miracle. You couldn't have convinced me for one second otherwise. Now I think, what a glorious way to be welcomed home into heaven than being surrounded by loved ones who were worshiping the Most High. I hated to see his soul leave this earth then, but I'm in awe now that he will never have to suffer here again. At first, my thoughts were hazy and fuzzy, and I could only see what I wanted to see, but now I've found myself puzzle-piecing things together.

In those first few moments after my husband's passing, I eventually pulled myself together and walked outside to face the unknown. What was I supposed to say to the crowd that was still hanging out on the back patio, waiting for me to come out? I didn't know. There weren't any more tears to possibly have been shed by me after my raging roar and the initial aftermath sting, but everyone projected their sorrow and grief onto me through hurt-filled hugs, sad faces, and droopy moods. Instinctively, being the optimistic person, extreme extrovert, natural fixer, and empathetic person that I am, I wanted to cheer everyone up instead of sitting in what I perceived as a dark, yucky space. I ventured to toss out a dry joke here and there, but the atmosphere was too complex. Was attempting to make people smile the *appropriate* thing to do at that place and time? I don't know.

Going through a valley such as this changes a person. Shortly after he had passed, one of my closest friends told me for the first time since knowing me that she didn't know who I was, how I was feeling, or what I was about to become. A few others questioned my heartbreak and love for Cody—to my face and behind my back— because they were not seeing the madness of grief that I chose to leave behind closed doors. The positive side of me that I was allowing them to see wasn't reacting the way they thought I should. They didn't know I was striving to seek hope in what they thought was despair.

After conversations with many other grievers, I learned that many of these people face similar trials when it comes to others inserting themselves where they shouldn't. The saying that death brings out the best and worst in people is true. My experiences also taught me that people near and far will always find a way to shame another for the actions and decisions they are making during such a vulnerable, incomprehensible time. Does that make these decisions right or wrong? I don't know. But I do know one thing: any decision right or wrong is not for any human to judge or condemn. That's God's job. Truth is, if one is worried about what's on my front porch, they're ignoring the garbage on their own. Everyone has a laundry list of sin because we are all dirty, wrinkled, and twisted crooks living in a broken, fallen world. Dare not cast a stone unless you're living a sinless life. "And Jesus said, 'Let him who is without sin among you be the first to throw a stone at her'" (John 8:7).

No two people will experience grief the same because each relationship with whom the person they lost was different in its own unique way. Someone may have lost a spouse, child, father, mother, grandparent, brother, sister, friend, etc., but those relationships all consisted of different levels and avenues. Some may have been extremely close with whom they lost, while others may not have had a super detailed or complex relationship. Some relationships may have been diverse or well-rounded, while others were surface level. A sudden, unexpected passing may have happened, while for others it's over the course of a long period of time. Each level of faith in an individual is different, too. Some people fear leaving this world, while others embrace it, so be it to whatever comes.

As a person who wears my heart on my sleeve at all times, no one seemed to know how to take me in the days to come. I processed solo, away from others. And writing helped me tremendously. No one knew how I'd face a hardship such as this. Often, I felt like eyes were watching my every move, waiting on me to crack and crumble. A major part of my identity had become Cody's partner and Mrs. Eubanks, and now that had been instantly ripped away, forcing myself to recreate my goals, visions, and realistic wants for the future. Finding my new identity and discovering more of who I am as an individual is a process in and of itself.

How were we supposed to move forward and proceed? How was I supposed to move forward and proceed? No one knew, but ultimately it's on us as individuals to figure it out for ourselves. The best advice I was given was to trust myself because nobody knows me like I know me. Unless I was to inflict harm upon myself or others, only I know what I need to get through this time. Some people need to be surrounded by their friends and families, while others need all the sleep and food they can get. Some need alone time and a quiet space for thinking, while others need worship and a spiritual atmosphere.

Realistically, everyone will leave this earth one day when we least expect it. But that doesn't mean everyone will handle being left behind the same. *One's perception is their reality and not all perceptions are the same, so not all realities are either.* No matter the dynamic of the relationship some may have had with Cody, it was still *different* than mine. In saying this, everyone expresses grief differently.

Personally, I needed quality time with the Lord and Cody's thick spiritual presence guiding my days. I needed the Word of Christ to encourage me that He's the only one I should be listening to. He reminds me that others are grieving, too. I needed game nights full of laughter surrounded by friends who let me be and do whatever I needed to be and do in that moment in time. Yet, I needed to isolate myself in order to recharge, too. I needed to feel comfortable and confident in my own decisions moving forward. I needed to remind myself over and over how temporary this life is compared to eternity. I needed to fully grasp that this world is not my home. I needed the escape of writing this book to relive each detail to help process it a tad bit slower this time. I needed to experience hope in having a future again someday. I needed the ways of this world to tell me "No!" so that Christ could scream back "Yes!" I needed those who were not meant to walk this next season with me to taper and fade off so that I could boldly step into my next chapter with those willing to cheer me on, flaws and all. I needed to see that despite my hurt in losing my husband, this world sadly would go on. And finally, I needed to know that God truly does have a plan for my short life left on this earth and that Cody will always be a part of it.

My advice to those who know people who are grieving is to be gracefully patient with them. Respect that they are doing what's best for them at the time. Love them despite their decisions that may not align exactly with what you think yours would be like during such a volatile, vulnerable time. Consciously pay attention to what they're really trying to express. And last, be lovingly intentional in conveying how much you care.

I encourage those who are grieving to do the same. Be patient with yourself. Listen to yourself and allow yourself to feel and absorb each emotion that comes. Pray more and seek refuge in the supernatural strength that only God can give. Trust yourself and your needs, while also allowing those who truly know you to fill your empty glass back up to the brim. Stomp on evil's head, speak truth and life, and take back the joy and happiness that the universe offers.

It's okay to be sad and have bad days, just don't dwell there for too long. He wants us to thrive! It's okay if people disagree with how you're handling yourself. They may not realize that getting in and out of bed in itself is a chore sometimes. But I'm proud of you. And so are many others. Believe it or not, there are also more people rooting for your blessings than you think. Don't let the enemy trick you into thinking that everybody is against you. Remember that you are never alone through your heartaches, flaws, or trials—Psalm 34:18. I encourage you to keep going despite not having it all together. Completely press into Him, and I promise He will hold you upright. His love is the greatest comfort I have ever experienced, and I want that for each of you, too. Remember that you are so loved by many, especially from the One whose love is ultimate. And don't forget John 13:7, "What I am doing you do not understand now, but afterwards you will understand!"

chapter twenty-five

I Am Blessed

Finding joy in this world again after losing a loved one, let alone your very best friend on the planet, is brutally difficult. But even in the brokenness, I am blessed and being pursued by divine intervention and supernatural love. With the help of my God and close family and friends who know me well and have chosen to walk beside me through it all, I've learned to truly listen to my body and my soul. If I feel led to lie in bed all day, I simply do just that, recharging myself for what tomorrow may bring. If I know I need to get out to appease my extrovert nature, I push the envelope and go, because I know it's what I need, to avoid sinking into a dark mental space. Perhaps leaving the house is not always only for me, but for others to witness.

I was once at such a high point in my life. Loving our Lord and this life to the fullest. Newly married, and still experiencing that burning puppy love between me and my groom. Blessed with an amazing marriage and perceivably healthy bodies, hobbies, and habits. I had my entire life with the person of my wildest dreams ahead of me, and we had recently moved into a stunning new home together, while attempting to expand our beautiful family. We were both thriving in our careers while helping other families achieve abundance, too. Cody and I never saw the cancer curveball coming. But there's a reason Christ allowed evil to put us to the test.

We often prayed for God to use us in a mighty way as long as we roamed this earth. We prayed that, if we were to be here, He would magnify Himself through us and use us as He saw fit. We vowed to be willing vessels for the glory of expanding His kingdom. Our hearts would sing a joyful melody that the band Passion expresses perfectly through their song "More Like Jesus." Christ saw fit to give us this battle because He knew, when we did not, that we would continue to shine light on His name and give Him glory despite taking everything. He allowed my husband, my sacred person, my *everything* to be taken from this world. He took all that I had, giving me no choice but to *make me more like Jesus* in knowing that our story would draw not only my heart but more hearts closer to Him.

Are you familiar with the story of Job in the Bible? If not, here are my CliffNotes. Job was a remarkable, upright man after God's own heart. He was godly, innocent, righteous, and humble. He rebuked evil and lived his life walking alongside the Lord. He was blessed with a wife, many children, servants, and livestock.

He was very wealthy and a great man by the world's standards. His life was considered picture-perfect, because this man had it all. Unfortunately, Job experienced ultimate human suffering at the hands of the devil. He lost *everything*. This man mourned, but still chose to continue worshiping the King. God knew all along that he would remain loyal to the Throne despite any obstacle thrown in his direction. Now that's admirable, unshakable faith! If Job can lose it all and still put his trust in the Big Man upstairs, so can I! Just like my Cody, Job seemed untouchable and invincible to the human eye, but the Lord often gives His strongest soldiers the toughest battles.

This reality affects many people in countless ways, but it taught me the harsh lesson to live each day as though it's my last and to be extra thankful for what I do have. Cherish the good times, forgive and recover quickly from the bad ones. Spend my valuable time in atmospheres that bring me joy. And it taught me to focus on things I can control rather than the things I cannot. It pressed me to dive into Scripture and find out what He says to be true. Do I, or will I, display this perfectly always? Absolutely not. However, in the grand scheme of things, I've come to realize that our life on earth is on borrowed time. I am here on purpose, and I must live on a mission for whatever the good Lord calls me to do. If I can use *this* tragedy to guide and point people to Christ, that's what I must do.

Several people have asked me if I have made peace with my husband's passing. My answer is simple: I made peace the day Cody went to heaven. I stand behind this answer, and here's why: I was and still am overwhelmed with thankfulness. Out of all the seven billion people on this planet, God matched me with him. I could have met and been with anyone in the world, but they would not have been my special Cody. And once again, he was insanely *special*. Our relationship was not flawless, but our connection was damn near perfect. We did not always see eye to eye, but we accepted and loved one another despite our flaws. I am beyond honored to have been given a life and love with him so deep, genuine, meaningful, and true.

Make no mistake about it, I was not by any means thankful that he passed. My heart still aches every day without my soul mate physically here with me, and I miss him so much that it hurts. If I could have it my way, I would choose to have him back by my side again and again and again and again and again. If love was enough to have kept him here, he would have remained here forever.

Unfortunately, many people these days will never be able to experience a love so pure. But I consider myself extremely blessed to have been able to experience such a remarkable love in this lifetime. *What was our secret?* you may ask. That answer is simple, too. We strived to keep Christ and His Word as the center of our union.

Out of respect to Cody, I must keep moving forward. I know that is what he would want for me and vice versa if the roles were reversed. He even told me this before he passed. In the journal I received, one of my questions to him was "How should I honor you?" His response was, "You tell me, but don't you be crying all of the time." This man melted me. He always knew exactly what to say.

Some people have made unruly comments that I did not love Cody enough because my outward grief does not consist of lying around, stuffing my face full of chocolates, sobbing or complaining all of the time. This is the most backwards mentality ever! What these same people with this mindset didn't see until now was the four long months we battled together, and the anguish I felt over the possibility of losing him. They couldn't see the way we looked at one another and longed for one another's company, always. They did not know that I never left his side when others did, and that I did everything I could at the time to ensure he was properly taken care of. I was there for *everything*. They didn't see me pull over on the side of the road in the middle of nowhere to let out all the tears before facing the public. They didn't witness the sleepless nights of me staying up with him, praying for him, and missing him. They didn't notice the meals not eaten and all the weight I really couldn't afford to lose since his diagnosis. They didn't see me literally lifting and carrying my husband with all of my might when he was too weak to support himself. They didn't follow me to the cemetery during all hours of the night, bawling my eyes out while missing his tender touch and soothing voice. They weren't there to help me off of the floor after begging God for more answers on how I should continue on now that we are no longer bound together through marriage. They weren't around to know how long it took, and sometimes it still takes me, to pull myself out of bed in the mornings, paralyzed from the trauma I just endured.

They did not see until now how much time and energy I've devoted to this book and The Eubanks Foundation in honor of my husband's story, legacy, and impact. They did not see our fiery passion for the King of the universe and that He still lives strong inside of me. And so on and so on. God needed Cody far greater than I did, because we fought for his life and we fought hard. It's because I love him so very much and our connection is so close that I am able to rejoice and celebrate his life and what is to come, despite my fleshly pain. I am confident that I will see him again standing beside Jesus, and it will be even more glorious than before.

My joy is not based on where I am at or these current circumstances. But my peace is found in whose I am and what is to come. Mercifully, the Lord has called me to be his daughter. I have witnessed unwavering submission towards Him through my beloved husband, not only on the hilltops but in the lowest of valleys. Therefore, I have been inspired to follow my King for life. This has allowed me to set my anchor on Him. If I had set my anchor on the things of this world, whether it be my career, money, relationships, or loving the life I had with Cody more than my love for the Lord, when the storm of life approached my doorstep, it could've easily swept me away. Tears may be rolling down my cheeks and my nose may be stuffed full of snot, but I hold confidence in knowing my hope is found in a rock that is secure. I am anchored to the God of the Most High! I follow and worship the only kingdom that has reigned forever! Placing my anchor in Him *isn't just to save* me through the storm, but *it is able to sustain* me through the storm. He won't just get me over trials and hardships, but He will walk with me in the middle of them. When I say that the praying sustained me, I mean it. Christ alone has held me as upright as possible through them. I'm not saying there aren't dark or sad moments. But for the most part, He has allowed me to focus on the good memories of mine and Cody's time together, as well as what the future holds, instead of dwelling on the gloomy days.

Oftentimes, I am blessed enough to take the dark and disruptive thoughts captive and obey Christ. Through prayer and keeping my eyes focused on what the Lord says about this situation, I have been able to raise those thoughts up with the knowledge of God. *Does this line up with the Holy Word? What does He say about these situations? What aroma am I giving off to others? Do I smell like death and hopelessness, or do I breathe life and prosperity?*

I have hope, eternal hope. Hope that one day I will be reunited with my brother in Christ in heaven under the authority of Jesus. This surely does not make the heartbreak of his passing any less painful, but it does make his worldly passing easier to understand. *Just because one may seem to carry the pain well does not mean it isn't still heavy.*

The Holy Bible simply gives knowledge to anyone who desires to know, to prepare ourselves that this world has to get a whole lot worse before prophecy can be fulfilled, and Christ will return. If this world were all goody-goody gumdrops and perfect all of the time, our vision would be clouded. We wouldn't look forward to Jesus's return if we had it made here, right? In heaven there will be no more sorrow, no more pain, and no more questions. His promises in John 16 are absolutely phenomenal, in case you need more reassurance and elaboration on this.

I *idolized* my husband, but I have to remember that *my* Cody was never mine to begin with. I was just entirely blessed enough to receive him for the short time that we had together. I find comfort in knowing that if God could sacrifice His only precious, perfect Son for the glory of His kingdom, surely I can do this for my forever love, too. Cody made it to where we are all aspiring to be someday. And I am so proud of him. I am excited that he is with Jesus in a place far greater than here. He will never be just a memory or a time period in my earthly life. He will always be a part of me, because our story together is a part of my testimony.

Jesus did not die in vain, therefore I cannot allow Cody's death to be in vain. While on this earth, he strived to serve our mighty King, and therefore this story had to be told to all who were and are willing to listen.

Xoxo

—Jackie